THE HISTORIES OF EUROPE

A Concise History of Brittany

This book is due for return on or before the last date shown below.

Series Editor

George Jones

Aberystwyth University

For other titles in this series, please see the University of Wales website:
www.uwp.ac.uk

THE HISTORIES OF EUROPE

A Concise History of Brittany

GWENNO PIETTE

UNIVERSITY OF WALES PRESS
CARDIFF
2008

www.uwp.co.uk

British Library Cataloguing-in-Publication Data
A catalogue record for this book is available from the British Library.

ISBN hardback 978-0-7083-2037-2
ISBN paperback 978-0-7083-2036-5

Typeset by Kerrypress Ltd, Luton, Beds
Printed in Malta by Gutenberg Press Ltd

Contents

Series Editor's Foreword   vii

Acknowledgements   ix

List of illustrations   x

Introduction   1

1   Prehistoric Armorica to the end of Roman domination (5000 BC – AD 420)   3

2   The British immigrations and the establishment of a Breton kingdom (AD 450–950)   19

3   Brittany becomes a duchy (936–1341)   36

4   The War of Succession and the end of the duchy (1341–1532)   49

5   Golden age and civil war (1532–1676)   63

6   Economic decline and the onset of the Revolution (1670–1789)   75

7   Revolution and counter-revolution (1789–1815)   87

8   Emigration, religion and language (1815–1914)   102

9   From the Great War to the eve of the Second World War (1914–39)   113

10 The Second World War to the present day   123

Bibliography   139

Index   143

Series Editor's Foreword

This series is intended to introduce the general reader to the histories of those parts of Europe which, despite having on at least some level or at some point in time their own 'national' identity, do not have their own present-day independent nation state or have only recently gained such a state. Many of them will be, therefore, in terms of the political reality and also in the minds of many, merely 'regions' of some larger national entity. One does not have to look far beneath the surface, however, to find that this is, to admittedly widely varying degrees, a contested issue. The questions of language, identity and politics that pertain to 'regions' or 'nations' in this situation frequently have some special characteristics of their own, including, in many cases, the implications of the efforts to construct and maintain national identity, for the most part in the face of opposition from the nation state concerned; the issues attendant on attempts to attain increased political autonomy or full independence; and the questions surrounding cultural, linguistic and political practices and principles at play where parts of Europe are inhabited by minorities whose identity differs in some way from the national majority.

The temporal scope of volumes in the series is wide. While the various authors may choose to place greater emphasis on some periods than others, depending on what is seen as being of the greatest importance and interest, the present volume takes a comprehensive approach and leads us from prehistory to the present day, including, amongst much else, the Roman period, the settlement by British immigrants, Brittany's period as a duchy and the effects of the French Revolution.

The disputed nature, referred to above, of the situations dealt with in this series (Brittany certainly being no exception, perhaps especially in terms of the impact of the Second World War and its aftermath on Breton identity and consciousness) demand of an author that s/he be objective without draining the life from what are in fact fascinating and engaging histories. This together with a grounding in a wealth of detailed fact has indeed been the strength of Dr Gwenno Piette's approach. We are fortunate to be able to include a volume on Brittany by one as intimately acquainted with that country as she is and it is a source of gratification that the solid start made by Dr Sharif Gemie, who furnished the volume on the history of Galicia (2006) and Dr Bernard Deacon who undertook the one on Cornwall (2007) has been maintained here.

George Jones

Acknowledgements

I wish to express my thanks to my family and friends for their support, encouragement and infinite patience during the writing of this book.

A special thank you to Steve Smith, proof reader, map maker, photographer and chauffeur.

List of illustrations

Plate 1 – Map of Brittany
Plate 2 – Roman temple at Corseul
Plate 3 – Close-up of Roman temple
Plate 4 – Statute of Nominoé
Plate 5 – Medieval street in Dinan
Plate 6 – Saint-Saveur de Redon abbey
Plate 7 – Suscinio castle
Plate 8 – Calvary cross at Guéhenno
Plate 9 – St Armel Church, Ploërmel
Plate 10 – Pierre Guillemot's house
Plate 11 – Summer villa in Dinard
Plate 12 – National First World War Monument
Plate 13 – Detail of frieze on monument

To my father

Arzel Even

Introduction

This concise history of Brittany encompasses the period from the early Neolithic times to the present day and inevitably certain personages and events have had to be omitted, but it is hoped nevertheless that this volume provides a comprehensive overview of what is a rich and varied history. The earlier chapters, dealing with events such as the Roman invasion, the British occupation and the establishment of the duchy, treat Brittany as the independent political entity it once was, but once Brittany was fully integrated into the kingdom of France the fortunes of the two countries become intertwined. So, while maintaining the emphasis on Breton history, the French historical context is also explained where necessary. It is because of this absorption that the focus shifts in the latter part of the book to the economy and culture of Brittany, as Paris increasingly became the centre stage for political events. The Breton movement is also discussed briefly in the final three chapters. Albeit involving only a small minority of the population, this is an element that has contributed to the uniqueness of Brittany and has played a part in preventing the country from simply evolving into a completely assimilated French province.

Geographically Brittany has traditionally been divided into east and west, Upper and Lower, and this division is reflected to a large extent in the linguistic history of the country. Even during the time of the Roman occupation there may have been linguistic differences as the Upper Bretons were more influenced by Roman customs entering from the east than their western brothers who continued to speak Gaulish. When the British came to settle in the peninsula during the first millennium AD it was Lower Brittany that was chosen as their base and their language, which developed into Breton, seems to have largely displaced Gaulish. For some people today Breton is the true language of

Brittany, but it should be noted that, despite the initial domination of those early British descendants, Breton never became the language of Upper Brittany. The people here developed their own language, Gallo. Nevertheless, Breton was at one time the language of the ruling elite and it was spoken by the vast majority in the west until the nineteenth century. It is in deference to this language that all place names in this book when first mentioned have the Breton version, if one exists, included in brackets.

Breton history has witnessed divisions other than linguistic within its borders and it has been racked by civil war more than once. Even after the consolidation of the duchy and the elimination of powerful fiefs, the country was torn in two during the War of Succession in the fourteenth century and the League Wars in the sixteenth. But arguably it was during the aftermath of the French Revolution, in the late eighteenth century, that Brittany found itself most divided. Ignoring any linguistic differences the country was split into various factions as certain areas and social classes supported the republic – while others both Breton and French speaking – violently opposed the revolution. Brittany is a place of contradictions, for example its people are often portrayed as devout Catholics willing to fight for their religious rights but this is also the place where the first communist mayor of France was elected. In a similar vein Brittany has been viewed by some as the mainstay of the *Résistance* during the Second World War, while for others it is a country of collaborators. This history therefore is also an attempt to describe and explain these contradictions and divisions while providing what is hoped is an intelligible and enjoyable narrative.

1

Prehistoric Armorica to the end of Roman domination (5000 BC – AD 420)

The peninsula of Armorica, the classical name for Brittany (*Breizh*), has a rich prehistory. The earliest evidence of humans is in the form of primitive stone tools dating from 700,000 years BC. The earliest settlement found, at Saint-Colomban, near Carnac (*Karnag*) dates back to 300,000 BC but it is the impressive number of Neolithic remains (5000 BC to 2000 BC) that is most striking. From majestic standing stones to beautifully engraved passage graves Brittany, for its size, has more megalithic monuments than anywhere else in Europe.

The most famous of these are the stone avenues near Carnac that extend for nearly three kilometres. Row upon row of standing stones varying in height from half a metre to four metres extend as far as the eye can see, with some stones veering off to form semi-circles and semi-rectangular enclosures. Numerous theories abound as to the purpose of this vast Neolithic construction. Was it a lunar observatory, an astronomical calendar, or a place for ritual ceremonies? We may never know, but these ancient and mysterious stones are awe-inspiring.

This Neolithic period of stone monuments and complex graves has been referred to as 'The Golden Age of Armorica' due to the abundance of gold objects unearthed, the most famous of these being the armlets found in a grave at Rondossec. Two-fifths of all the prehistoric gold items discovered in France have been located in Brittany. This was also a time of a flourishing trade in polished stone axes that were exported in huge quantities along the rivers Loire (*al Liger*), Seine and Rhône. Breton polished axes of this period have been discovered as far apart as Belgium and southern Britain.

Brittany continued to flourish during the Bronze Age (2,000 to 900 BC) and the peninsula developed its trading routes, importing gold from Ireland, silver from Spain and tin from Britain. It exported bronze tools, swords and artefacts to Germany and the Netherlands. However, towards the end of the Bronze Age there seems to have been something of a crisis. This has been surmised because of the increasing number of hoards found dating from 800 to 700 BC. Burying, or throwing vast numbers of objects into a river, seems to have been a common custom in prehistoric times and archaeologists have suggested that this practice may have been a form of religious offering. The hoards comprise of many different items but the main content is axes. Several of these axes have never been used and others have such a high lead content, or were made so thinly, that they would have been useless as tools or weapons. It has been suggested that the latter were expressly manufactured for the purpose of being buried in a hoard. The seventh and eighth centuries BC were a time of political upheaval in Europe. The rise of the Greeks and Etruscans in the south and the Hallstatt culture in central Europe caused the main trade routes to shift eastwards much to the detriment of the Atlantic sea routes of which Brittany was a part. Moreover, Brittany was still using obsolete bronze technology at a time when most of the rest of Europe was using iron. Brittany, still manufacturing outdated and unwanted products, was becoming increasingly isolated. It has been suggested that the increased number of hoards can be interpreted as a desperate attempt to appease the gods in a time of economic crisis.

Eventually Brittany did adapt and the country began to develop its own iron industry and thus entered the Iron Age. From this time onwards, the mid-fifth century BC, it is possible to regard the people living in Brittany as Celtic in the sense that they spoke a proto-Celtic language. They had close connections and similarities with the cultures of other so-called Celtic peoples and showed Celtic features in their art. At one time it was believed that Celtic tribes from central Europe invaded western Europe bringing their culture and knowledge of iron technology with them. However, skeletal material from Brittany, Normandy and the Paris basin has shown that there is no evidence of any mass migration from the east between Neolithic times and the ninth century AD. It would seem therefore that Brittany became

Celtic when its own evolving culture became influenced by external cultural developments.

By the late fifth century and early fourth century BC the Armorican peninsula was divided into five tribal chiefdoms, the most famous of which are the Veneti. This tribe lived roughly in the area of the modern *département* of Morbihan, an area which, according to archaeological evidence, had always been the richest part of the country. Bountiful seas and fertile land helped this coastal area to develop. The Veneti were the most powerful of the tribes and they were the first, in the second century BC, to mint coins made of gold and silver alloy. Their coins were thick and heavy and of good quality and although they were essentially copies of a Greek design they produced their own artistic versions featuring human heads with elaborate hairstyles, horses and charioteers.

Brittany continued developing as a rural community and with the introduction of iron more and more forest was cleared for the plough (modern aerial photography shows just how densely populated this land became). Although there were no towns to speak of, each tribe, from the second century onwards, did have a centre, essentially a fortified settlement, where the chief was based. The Veneti's centre was *Darioritum* which evolved into modern day Vannes (*Gwened*). The Veneti were excellent sailors and traded along the treacherous Breton coasts. As Brittany was drawn more and more into the Roman Empire's orbit the Veneti became important middlemen for transporting Roman goods across the channel to Britain. Trade in wine was brisk; like all the Gauls, the Armoricans were extremely partial to wine and apparently the going rate for an amphora of wine, 25 litres, was one slave.

Julius Caesar claimed that the Veneti had sole control over the cross-channel routes but archaeological evidence suggests that this was not always the case. Most of the Armorican coins found in Britain have not been Venetic but rather they derive from another tribe, the Coriosolitae. This tribe controlled the territory between the central forest and the northern coast, corresponding to the eastern half of the modern *département* of Côtes-d'Armor

(*Aodoù-an-Arvor*). As inhabitants of the north coast it is logical
that the Coriosolitae should have looked to Britain for trading
opportunities. Pottery made in the region of the Bay of
Saint-Brieuc (*Sant-Brieg*), along with amphorae shards, have
been found on the Channel Islands and at Hengistbury Head,
which was the major port of entry on the Solent coast at that time.
The inference is that the Coriosolitae transported Italian wine,
together with local produce, inside locally made containers to
Hengistbury, calling at Guernsey on the way. However, the wine
was probably traded with the Veneti first, who then conveyed the
amphorae up to the Coriosolitae, either around the coast or along
inland rivers. The fact that the Coriosolitae were relatively late in
minting their copper and silver alloy coins (90–80 BC) may
suggest that before then they were vassals of the Veneti who may
have controlled the trade routes along the inland rivers that
passed through Coriosolitae territory. Their coins were probably
minted at the port of Alet, on the mouth of the river Rance (*Ar
Renk*), which was the only pre-Roman settlement of any size.
Alet was important as a trading centre for goods moving to and
from Britain, but the Coriosolitae's tribal centre was at *Fanum
Martis*, modern Corseul (*Kersaout*).

The other tribe that occupied Brittany's northern coast was the
Osismi whose territory occupied the whole of the modern
département of Finistère (*Penn-ar-Bed*) and also extended
eastward to the river Ellé (*An Ele*) in the south east and the river
Gouët (*Ar Goued*) in the north east. Their tribal centre was
Vorgium, which is probably modern Carhaix (*Karaez*). The
Osismi minted gold coins of a light and inferior quality which
gradually debased into electrum, but the iconography was
unusual in that the human head turned to the left. Indeed, the
variety of different types of Osismi coins, unlike the other tribes
which each had an identifiable kind, and the scattered geographical distribution, suggests that these coins were struck for a
number of lesser chiefs or petty kings.

Apart from the sea the most important trading route into and
out of Brittany was the Loire river and the lands around the
mouth of this vast river were controlled by the Namnetes. They

had their centre, *Condevicnum*, where the rivers Loire and Erdre (*An Erzh*) meet; this is present day Nantes (*Naoned*).

Of the five tribes the smallest territory was occupied by the Redones and it corresponds roughly with the *département* of Ille-et-Vilaine (*Il-ha-Gwilen*). Their tribal centre was at *Condate*, modern Rennes (*Roazhon*). They began minting gold coins from about the third century BC onwards and their coins are identified by a horse with a stylized head and insectiform body. Most of the Armorican coins follow the basic pattern, a male head crowned with a laurel on one side, and a galloping horse driven by a charioteer with a whip and a wheel or a figure placed below the horse on the reverse side.

Armorican trade was thriving in the period immediately before the Roman conquest. Her exports may well have included iron or tin but the peninsula almost certainly sold salt and salted fish. Salt was an important commodity, used in the preservation of food and the curing of leather and there were numerous saltworks all along the coasts of Brittany, 120 of which have been identified. The salt would be collected from the beach after high tide and then washed in clean water. Once free of sand the salt solution would be evaporated in ovens to produce the salt. By the third century BC the process had become more sophisticated in that particular ovens had been developed that could heat 250 specially constructed salt-moulds at one time. As shards of these moulds have been found at inland settlements it would seem that the salt bars, shaped like truncated pyramids, were sold in their containers.

Most of Brittany's population lived along the coast in small settlements big enough for an extended family. These were open hamlets or farmsteads whose ditches and sturdy fences were designed to keep out wild animals rather than human enemy. But there were other settlements that were much more heavily fortified, located in easily defended sites such as hilltops and cliffs. Some of the larger inland hill forts were probably minor tribal centres, but others are situated in such desolate windswept places it is hard to envisage them as permanent settlements. They may have been places of refuge in difficult times, or a site for seasonal gatherings for a religious festival. On the coast, especially in Veneti territory, from the gulf of Morbihan to south Finistère, the 'cliff castles', as they have been called, were situated on headlands projecting into the sea. These were cut off from the land by a series of complex ditches and earthen ramparts, making the site virtually inaccessible. It was these promontory forts that were to prove such a headache for Julius Caesar when he attacked the Armorican peninsula.

The Romans had been gradually extending their empire in southern France during the second century BC and by 120 BC they controlled the Massif Central. They then consolidated their position by making treaties with the tribes of central Gaul and formed trading alliances. When Julius Caesar campaigned against Armorica in 57 BC he was basically completing the task of conquering Gaul but he may well have had the invasion of Britain already in his sights also.

Caesar's campaign is described in his *De Bello Gallico*, a vivid, albeit biased, eye-witness account of the events. Initially the invasion of 57 BC seemed to be a simple affair with the Armoricans quickly submitting to Caesar's young officer Publius Crassius, offering hostages as surety. That winter Crassius quartered his garrison near Angers but when he sent envoys the following spring to the Veneti and the Coriosolitae in order to claim the food and grain that had been promised in the peace treaty, the messengers were killed and the Armoricans demanded the release of their hostages. Rome's refusal was the excuse to start the revolt. Under the leadership of the Veneti the Armorican tribes united, along with other Celtic tribes situated in Normandy and reinforcements from Britain were sent for. Perhaps the docile submission the previous year was simply a ploy to obtain extra time for preparation.

Arriving in Gaul in late spring of 56 BC Caesar ordered a fleet of ships to be built along the Loire and he immediately attacked the Veneti leaving the subjugation of the tribes in Normandy and north Brittany to Sabinius. He also sent troops to Aquitania and the Belgic tribes in order to suppress any hint of rebellion there and to prevent them providing more reinforcements to help

Brittany. Caesar was now to find out how effective the Veneti promontory forts were at repelling the enemy. Impossible to reach from the land at high tide, at low tide the Roman ships simply floundered on the rocks. The times when the Romans did finally get close to gaining access, by building huge dykes to keep the sea away, the besieged garrison of the 'cliff castle' would load up anything of any worth on to their flat-keeled, high-sterned boats and slip away to the next promontory stronghold, leaving behind an empty shell. The deep indentations caused by the several estuaries, gorges and swamps and the wild rough seas on a virtually harbourless coast, made it extremely difficult for the Romans to pursue their enemy on land or sea. Caesar realized that the only way to win was to lure the Veneti into a sea battle once his ships were ready and this battle was fought in the bay of Quiberon (*Kiberen*) near St-Gildas-de-Rhuys (*Lokentaz*).

The Veneti ships, 220 of them according to *De Bello Gallico*, were large high vessels strongly built of oak with sails of skins and thin-dressed leather and anchors that fastened with iron chains rather than cables. The Roman ships were lighter and lower which made them more manoeuvrable, but they were no match against the Veneti ships, which were perfectly adapted to the rough seas and rocky coasts. The Romans' usual tactics of using the beak of their ships to pierce their enemies' hulls proved ineffective, as was their custom of building turrets on board from which to attack. The Veneti ships were too high and too strong but they lacked one essential feature – oars.

The beginning of the battle went well for the Veneti, but the tables turned when the wind suddenly dropped. The Veneti fleet was immobilized and the Romans were able to row up close and bring down their sails by means of long hooked poles. Realising that they were losing the Veneti fleet tried to flee, but again their progress was hampered by the lack of wind and the Romans picked them off one by one. The battle raged for eight hours and ended in complete victory for the Romans with many of the Veneti killing themselves or leaping into the sea to avoid capture and a life of slavery.

Caesar's testimony claims that most of the Armorican tribes were slaughtered or sold into captivity and the country, broken in spirit, was left in ruins. The evidence suggests otherwise. Very small bronze coins of a Gaulish style have been found in Veneti territory and near Morlaix (*Montroulez*) that date from immediately after the Roman conquest, which suggest that the native authorities still had some control. Gaulish place-names survived the occupation and even the Veneti's supposedly devastated centre's name, *Darioritum*, continued in use. Nor were all the Veneti ships necessarily destroyed, as *De Bello Gallico* would have us believe: the remains of Roman amphorae scattered on the Morbihan coast dating from the same period suggest that Veneti commerce continued, albeit under Roman surveillance.

Neither did the territorial boundaries change much although the Namnetes did lose their lands to the south of the Loire to the neighbouring tribe of the Pictones who were pro-Roman. Despite their resistance, the Armorican peoples do not in fact seem to have been treated any worse than any other vanquished tribe.

However, Brittany did not accept her colonial status within the Roman empire without some protest. When Vercingetorix led a general uprising in Gaul four years later, the Veneti, Coriosolitae, Redones and Osismi all supported him by sending troops to the great battle of Alesia that ended in disaster for the Gauls. The following year Armorican tribes rose up again, to support the Andecavi against the pro-Roman Pictones, but this insurgence ended in defeat as well. Resentment continued to simmer in the province as is vividly illustrated by a hoard of coins found in Port-Haliguen, Quiberon, dating to 8 BC, where, on all the Roman coins, the imperial effigy has been defaced. In fact, it took the Romans sixty years to subdue Gaul completely. The suppression of druidism in AD 21 saw yet another rebellion in northern Gaul and the destruction of public buildings at Quimper (*Kemper*) and Carhaix and of the native settlement at Alet testifies to the revolt spreading to Brittany also. Still, the Romanization of Brittany continued and, in fact, the province flourished under Roman rule.

Armorica was incorporated into the administrative system of Roman Gaul, becoming part of the province of Lugdunensis and the administrative centres were based on the old tribal strongholds. These centres or *civitates* did not receive the same 'free' or 'federated' status like those of other cities who had willingly joined the Roman hegemony. Instead, they were *civitates stipendariae*, which meant that they were simply subjects of Rome. However, with time, these distinctions ceased to be relevant as the whole character of the empire became more uniform. Thus, there were five *civitates* in Brittany organising the taxes, administrating justice and maintaining law and order. The *civitates* were run by executive officers who were elected for one year by an assembly of leading citizens. Most of these were native Armoricans, powerful local men who had become Roman citizens and were fully integrated into Roman society.

The *civitates* were responsible for the territory corresponding to the old tribal territory that was further divided into smaller units called *pagi*. Many of these tribal subdivisions reflected local loyalties and identities within the larger community and they form the basis of the modern *pays* which can still incite fierce passions today (for example pays Bigouden with its distinctive traditional headdress).

The administrative centres based in *civitates* developed into Roman towns, with regular street grids and amenities such as public baths, administrative buildings and theatres. *Condate* (Rennes) was constructed according to an orthogonal plan and by the early second century it had huge baths, a basilica, a temple to Mars Mallo, suburban villas and pottery workshops. Other towns developed, such as the main centres of a *pagi*, or around a river ford and these townships, although not formally planned, still had Roman features such as the theatre at Locmariaquer (*Lokmaria-Ker*). However, the cities in Armorica did not develop the way those located more centrally in Gaul did. The towns were small and few in number and this is reflected in the number of theatres. Gaul as a whole had over a 100 stone-built theatres, but Brittany only had two – in Locmariaquer and Nantes. There may have been wooden theatres also which have since perished but, even so, the fact remains that the towns did not develop to any great extent.

While the *civitates* were mostly administrative in role the real wealth was in the countryside, on the agricultural estates or *fundus*. They extended over 200–300 hectares and employed or maintained hundreds of people. The main produce that was farmed was wheat, but flax and hemp were also grown and all these were exported along with animal products. The proprietor was usually a rich Romanized Celt and the estate would be named after him. Some of these names have survived in communes and hamlets, for example Vitré (*Gwitreg*) is derived from *fundus Victorianus*, after the estate of *Victorius*. The country estate usually had a villa constructed for the proprietor and these were often richly furnished with mosaics, heated baths, frescos and fine pottery. The floors were sometimes laid with patterned slate and limestone slabs and the walls adorned with stucco arches and colonnades. Wall plaques carved with dolphins and sea-monsters were fashionable in the late second and early third centuries. Most of the wealthiest villas have been found along the coast, especially in the Morbihan, but there were villas on farmsteads inland also in the Rennes basin.

Romanized rural settlements have also been found in less welcoming places, such as desolate hilltops, rugged cliffs and small islands. These show how Roman fashions and techniques spread to the Armorican peasantry and how on smaller settlements also their Iron Age wooden farmsteads were being replaced with stone villas.

The grand estates produced surplus for export to towns and an effective network of communication was necessary for trade and to run the administrative centres. This was provided by the road system. The Roman road is famous but it seems that the road system developed by the Romans here was based on older Gaulish routes that they adapted. The network of roads in Brittany were part of the great road system throughout Gaul that radiated from the Gallo–Roman capital Lyon. There were three kinds of roads, the *viae militares* or *consulares* that were the main trunk roads, the secondary routes that united *civitates* to *civitates* and the *viae vicinales* that were the provincial byroads. The *viae militares* were used by the 'imperial post' – messengers who kept the outposts in touch with the rest of Gaul and Rome itself. The three major trunk roads in Brittany run east to west, the northern and southern routes running along the coastal plateaux but keeping inland of the indenting rias, while the central route runs lengthwise across the central depression. Stations were located along the *viae militares*. Every 48 or 50 km there were *mansiones*, the granary stores and every 12 or 15 km the *mutationes* provided fresh horses and lodgings. There were also regular *castella* where patrols kept watch to safeguard the imperial postal service and the granary stores and to quell brigandage. Along each Roman mile stood a milestone, some of them made of stone and some of wood.

No bridge dating from the Roman period has been found and so it seems that all the rivers were forded. Travellers would throw a coin into the water as they crossed in order to appease the water gods. Thirty thousand Roman coins from Augustus to Valentian II (AD 375–92) have been found in the river Vilaine at Rennes. Since fords were places where traffic had to slow down or even stop if the river was temporarily impassable or tidal, wine shops and various stalls appeared and here these developed into small townships. Many Breton towns like Morlaix, Landerneau (*Landerne*) and Quimperlé (*Kemperle*) began their life in this way during the Roman period.

The extensive network of roads in Brittany is witness to the density of the population. It also indicates the importance of certain towns. Thus, the six roads that connect Vannes with the other capitals show the importance of this city state and the extent of the relations of the Veneti with the rest of Gaul. The most important city of Roman Armorica, Carhaix, has more than seven roads leading from it.

The road system also linked up the main rivers and, in response, major ports developed on the estuaries such as *Condevicum* (Nantes) on the Loire and several little ports appeared along the coast, as in Quimper, for example. The new communication system had an effect on trade in that goods could now be exchanged to and exported from all over the country.

Brittany now imported Roman goods for local consumption and the developed road system meant that luxury goods could reach the remotest villa. Wine from Italy and olive oil from Spain continued to be important imports and marble was obtained from Greece, Italy and Tunisia. No doubt many other products of the Roman empire flowed into the province as demand increased with Romanization but archaeological data is limited to non-perishable material such as amphorae and pottery. The ability to buy these commodities, some of which were used to embellish villas and towns, signifies that Armorica must have had surplus goods for exchange. Again there is a dearth of evidence for what was actually exported by the peninsula but we can assume it would have included cereals, meat, salted fish and *garum* (see below).

Local trade between Brittany and Britain continued. The local shipmasters continued to ply back and forth transporting local products under Roman occupation just as their forefathers had done and some of them probably carried a few Roman goods in addition. But in fact, although internal trade along the roads and rivers became important as Brittany eagerly consumed Roman fashions, the overall amount of bulk goods decreased.

Before the Roman conquest the Atlantic seaway had been an important route for the moving of goods from the Roman empire to northern Gaul and onwards to Britain. Operating outside the empire Roman entrepreneurs could exploit the situation to their advantage and they made enormous profits. Once the Atlantic coast of Gaul was incorporated into the empire the merchants were no longer exempt from Roman taxes and regulations and many looked eastward beyond the frontier to continue their profitable trading along the southern North Sea. The route between Alet on the north coast of Brittany and Hengistbury on the south coast of England was no longer used for mass bulk goods and the archaeological evidence shows a sharp decline in wine amphorae. With the conquest of Britain and the growing importance of *Londinium*, it became even more advantageous to export goods along the North Sea and up the Thames estuary, especially as this Channel crossing was safer and quicker than sailing around the Armorican peninsula. Therefore, Armorican merchants were no longer the middlemen on the long trading routes; instead Armoricans had become consumers.

Garum sauce, mentioned above, was probably exported. This was a sauce made from salted fish and was a Roman delicacy that was popular throughout Europe. Salt collecting continued to be an important activity and the Iron Age salt-making hearths were replaced by more efficient Roman structures, such as the tiled kiln excavated at Camézon, Plonévez-Porzay (*Plonevez-Porzhe*). The industry was also extended, with the coasts around Douarnenez Bay now becoming a major salt-making centre. Other salt sites were in the bay of Saint-Brieuc (*Sant-Brieg*) and at Lorient (*An Oriant*). Vast numbers of massive fish-salting tanks appear from the second century onwards and testify to large-scale production suitable for export. The fish were mostly small sardines of which there were plenty in offshore waters. Fish paste and salted fish may well have been transported to export markets along with the *garum*. The techniques of the Armorican fish-salting industry are very similar to those of Morocco and southern Spain and the reference to a community of Roman citizens in Douarnenez in the second century (before all Armorican citizens were granted Roman citizenship in AD 211) suggests that this was not a locally inspired industry but one that was developed and run by 'foreign' entrepreneurs.

Brittany's mineral wealth continued to be exploited under the Romans although it remained on a small scale. The mining of alluvial tin deposits at Saint-Renan (*Lokournan*) in north-west Finistère and at the mouth of the Vilaine persisted, as did the lead mines in Plélauff (*Pellann*) in Côtes-d'Armor and Dorges-Crossac in Loire-Atlantique (*Liger-Atlantel*). Iron ore continued to be mined on a small scale and slag heaps dating back to the Roman times are found throughout Brittany.

Town planning, public baths and decorated villas are all examples of the willingness of the Armoricans to embrace Roman fashions and customs, but to what extent did the population become truly Romanized other than superficially? After all, there is a difference between economic integration and ideological assimilation and Brittany was in a remote corner of the empire. It should be noted that Romanization, such as it was, was uneven. Very few Roman inscriptions have been found in the west of the country and the new ideas and tastes penetrated here much more slowly than the eastern part and the areas in close contact with the major trading routes of the Loire. Awareness and adoption of new habits and fashions would also have been uneven according to rank and social class.

Gaulish, the Celtic language spoken on the continent, remained the main language of the inhabitants. Other than a few merchants, administrators and soldiers, the non-native element that settled in Brittany was minute. The study of personal names found on dedications and graffiti shows that the majority of the people had Celtic or Romanized Celtic names. The survival of Gaulish place names also testifies to the strength of the language. While the towns and some of the larger country estates may have had inhabitants who were bilingual in Gaulish and some form of Latin, the majority would have been monolingual Gaulish speakers.

Even the gods that the Romans brought with them were modified to suit Celtic customs. Mercury became *Lug*-Mercury and Mars was *Teutates*-Mars and many Roman–Celtic temples were built according to local styles and on the remains of pre-Roman sanctuaries. Statues and statuettes of Vulcan, Hercules, Minerva, Diana and Cupid have been found in Brittany but it is difficult to judge whether they had Celtic elements attributed to them as they are in classical dress.

The exception to this tendency to look for Celtic divine counterparts is the cult of the Spirit of Rome and the Emperor. There are numerous public and private dedications to *Numen* of the Emperor such as those found at Nantes, Rennes and Corseul. Other evidence points to the presence of Imperial cult priests in Rennes while bronze statuettes of Victoria (Victory) have been discovered in Carhaix, Kerlaz and Corseul.

There is some testimony that other non-Roman religions also found some adherents here. Bronze and gold statuettes of the Egyptian cult of Isis, Sapiris and their son Harpocrates have been discovered but no shrines or temples. There are also a few traces of the new faith of Christianity but, like the other 'foreign' religions, in urban contexts only and most people remained loyal to the old gods. Several places like the mountain top of Ménez-Hom (*Menez-C'homm*) continued to be venerated and the water cult devotional practice of throwing coins into streams continued. The native fertility cult was also dominant and pipe clay statuettes of mother-goddesses are common throughout the country. These cheap figurines of nursing mothers sitting in a chair and various types of naked goddesses were mass produced locally in Rennes, Tréguennec (*Tregeneg*) and elsewhere. They were intended for personal devotion in private chapels, as ex-voto in public shrines and were buried with the dead.

But whether all its inhabitants were fully Romanized or not, in general Brittany shared in the prosperity of the empire, especially during the century between the Emperors Nerva (AD 96) and Commodus (died AD 192). This was a period of economic growth and vitality. The *garum* and salt-fish industry was at its peak, new villas were built, towns were embellished – and this was all made possible by dynamic inter-provincial trading. In the latter half of the second century, however, this stable and prosperous situation came under threat sporadically. Raiders along the coast caused havoc and there may well have been internal unrest also. Some of the richer citizens of Quimper for example decided it was safer on their country estates and their private town dwellings fell into disuse. In other areas it was villas that were burned down, although some of these were rebuilt later.

During the third century the situation worsened considerably with attacks from without and within. Along the coast Frankish, Saxon and Frisian pirates were raiding the north of Gaul including Armorica and the lower Loire. On the other hand, there was internal political and military instability after the assassination of Emperor Gordian III in 244. Gaul was separated from the Roman empire for fourteen years as a result of the Postumus revolt in 260. This turbulent time is represented archaeologically by a number of coin hoards that were probably buried in a panic. In addition, coastal towns like Nantes, Brest, Alet and

Saint-Servan were fortified and even inland Rennes reinforced its defences. Towns were torched and villas abandoned. Trading links were severed causing the *garum* and salt-fish industry to decline until it stopped altogether. Vast tracts of the countryside could no longer be farmed efficiently and the forest began to recolonize the cleared land.

There was a brief respite at the beginning of the fourth century AD when Emperor Diocletian (284–305) made valiant efforts to hold back the barbarian onslaught on the frontiers of Roman Europe. Armorica became part of a defensive interconnecting system of forts and naval bases that stretched from the straits of Dover to the mouth of the Gironde. Sheltered behind high walls in urban areas and protected by garrisons at sea and on land, the population began to recover. But this period of relative stability came to an end with the usurpation of Emperor Magnentius in 350 followed by the barbarian attack on the Rhine two years later. The situation deteriorated rapidly thereafter as the coin economy reverted to barter, all the villas were abandoned and the Roman way of life was becoming increasingly unsustainable. Finally, the Armoricans realized that the Roman empire was no longer relevant. It could not protect them from barbarian attacks and peasant revolts, or provide for them economically and so, in the second decade of the fifth century, the Armoricans established their own system of administration and expelled the Roman governors.

The Roman period of Brittany had come to an end.

2

The British immigrations and the establishment of a Breton kingdom (AD 450–950)

During the next phase of its history Brittany underwent a fundamental change that meant that by the sixth century much of the country was controlled and populated by a new people. When and why they came, and whether they displaced the native population, is open to debate, but there is no question about the origin of these newcomers. They hailed from south-west Britain. Modern Breton is derived from insular Celtic British, not continental Gaulish, and an examination of a modern map reveals place names in Brittany which are remarkably similar to those in Wales and Cornwall. Some, like Trégastel / Trecastell and Gwendraezh / Gwendraeth, reflect the close linguistic relationship, while others, such as Lanildut (*Lannildud*) / Llanilltud Faerdre and Landéleau (*Landelo*) / Llandeilo share the personal names of saints, Illtud and Teilo in these cases. Such was the influence of the immigrants that by the end of the sixth century Armorica had a new name: *Britannia* was now the standard Latin term for the peninsula.

Throughout the Middle Ages there was a strong awareness of the close ties between south-west Britain and Brittany and this is echoed in various legends and saints' lives, which describe, sometimes in graphic detail, the Britons' arrival in Brittany. While illustrating the basic fact that the country was colonized by Britons, these colourful texts, written for the most part centuries later, must be viewed with extreme caution before they are treated as valid historical sources.

Approaching the peninsula from the west and landing on the northern shores, the Britons had dominated the west and the north of Brittany probably since the middle of the fifth century.

Recent developments in archaeological evidence suggest that the British migrants may have started to settle here earlier than hitherto thought. They may even have first arrived towards the end of the third century, while Armorica was still nominally under Roman control. As described in the previous chapter the third century was a time of upheaval with pirate attacks, peasant uprisings, looting bandits; and many villas and farms were abandoned. Some of these rural sites were subsequently reoccupied but the behaviour of the new residents suggests that they were a different people altogether. They regularly rejected the existing buildings and sometimes even demolished them and generally they seem to have avoided the Roman-built roads and Gallo–Roman towns and centres.

It is virtually impossible to say exactly how many Britons landed on the shores of Brittany with the intent of settling there but the general picture that is emerging is that of the first immigrants possibly arriving in a trickle in the third century, while their numbers increased greatly in the fourth. The immigration may have continued, in one form or another, until the ninth century.

British Celts were no strangers to Brittany; traders' ships had been plying the sea between the island and the peninsula for generations, since well before Roman times, and now that some of the British were intent on stopping over it has been suggested that they were welcomed by the Armoricans and, sharing a similar language and culture, integrated easily. It is true that no evidence has been unearthed as yet that displays signs of resistance to or conflict with the British immigrants in the west of the country. On the other hand, place-name studies, along with the existing archaeological data, imply that in fact, in many places, there was very little contact with the native population. Excavations at a burial site in St Urnel-en-Plomeur (Cap Sizun – south of Douarnenez), whose earliest remains date to AD 320–80, disclosed skeletons of people whose cranial measurements indicate that they came originally from south-west Britain. These anthropological characteristics are identical to those of the population of Cap Sizun during the Middle Ages, thus proving that these south-west British characteristics were not diluted in any way for a number of centuries. This would suggest that there had been no inter-marriage with the local population at all, if indeed there was a local population to be had as the fact that so many place names were replaced with new British ones may indicate that there was no-one around to tell the newcomers what places were called. The names of once important cities were forgotten so that *Vorgium* (Carhaix) was now dubbed simply as 'the town', and even rivers were bestowed with new names.

So what happened to the native Armoricans, the Gallo–Romans? While villas and farms inland were being abandoned and pollen analysis has shown that there was a decline in agriculture, the cities along the shores increased in size and the few Gaulish and Roman place-names that have survived are mainly along the coast also; for example the village of Argol (which is about 5 km from the sea) derives its name from *Agricola*. Gallo–Roman enclaves certainly existed in the sea of British: we know that Locmaria (*Lokmaria*), now a suburb of Quimper, retained its Latin name of *Aquilonia Civitas* until the eleventh century, and that Latin and later a Romance language, was also spoken in this area, which includes Quimper and Briec-sur-l'Odet (*Brieg*), until the eleventh century. There is no real evidence of any mass movement of population but in general it would seem that, while a number of Gallo–Romans obviously did leave the country for the town, there may well have been a decline in their population as well as a consequence of the deteriorating living conditions.

The situation was different in south-east Brittany. Gaulish place names, often ending in '-ac', are much more numerous here and not all the villas were abandoned permanently. Some of the farmsteads were rebuilt and occasional sections of Roman roads were still in use also, in particular around Vannes. Sheltering behind their strong defensive walls Vannes, Rennes and Nantes may well have clung on to the Roman way of life for years after the rest of the country had succumbed to British dominance.

The colonizers may have reached the Vannetais region as early as the fifth century, and they had certainly done so by the sixth and seventh. They must have come into contact with the native population this time and their progress here does seem to be slower than in the north and west. Nevertheless, by the end of the ninth century most of the personal and place-names here were Breton. This signifies a language shift from Gaulish or Latin to Breton, but does not necessarily mean a population shift. The original inhabitants may have stayed put and learned the language of the newcomers.

If the Britons did indeed begin settling in the late third century it must have been with the Roman authorities' consent, because although the decline of the Empire had already set in, the Romans still had enough control in Gaul to have been able to prevent the newcomers from establishing themselves. This brings us to the question why did the Britons come in the first place. It should be mentioned that Britons migrated to other places in Europe about this time also, but it was only in Brittany that they were to have such a long-lasting effect on the language, social identity and political structure. The Britons may have been moving on because of raids by Irish and Pictish pirates, there may have been overpopulation and lack of land; but, given that the migration lasted until the ninth century the reasons were probably varied and numerous. One suggestion is that they were initially Romano–British troops being used in western Gaul in defence of the Empire who then stayed on, and were even encouraged to repopulate the abandoned areas. Still, it seems unlikely that the initial wave was military in any form as there is no mention of this in Roman records that usually include such military movements. According to one tradition, the British made their appearance when the Imperial pretender Maximus was defeated in 388 at the battle of the Save in Emona (in modern Slovenia). He returned to Britain, from where he came, but supposedly a certain number of his troops stayed behind and installed themselves in Armorica under the leadership of Conan Meriadec. Gildas, on the other hand, writing *De Excidio* in 540, claims that the Britons were fleeing the Anglo Saxons, but this is propaganda on Gildas's part as the Saxons were no threat in the west of Britain at this time.

It may well be significant that the burials at St Urnel appear to be Christian, the orientation of the tombs and the absence of artefacts implies this and this was a time before the Roman Empire had adopted Christianity officially. This might explain why the immigrants seemed to renounce the Roman way of life, as they rejected the villas, roads and existing towns. That there may have been a religious reason for the migration is borne out by the fact that many of the British leaders' names are now commemorated in place names as saints. Many of these 'saints' were members of aristocratic princely families, although some were spiritual leaders and heads of small monastic communities judging from the remains of small religious sites on wind-swept islands. They reorganized the country throughout in a methodical manner, and brought their institutions, laws and administrative procedures with them. They established a network of parishes, the 'plous', and disrupted the ecclesiastical framework of the late Roman empire. Although the Theodosican Code (AD 380), was implemented in Gaul, reorganizing the dioceses in keeping with the maxim of one bishop per *civitas*, most of Brittany's churches went their own way when it came to custom and traditions. Theoretically all the churches of Armorica came under the remit of the metropolitan see of Tours, but the sixth century bishops of Tours, Angers and Rennes failed to exercize control over Celtic practices such as portable altars, which had much in common with the Irish church.

Initially, there was no single political identity in what was now Breton Armorica. The country was divided into separate regions with Dumnonia in the north taking its name from the British tribe of Dommonii from Devon, while Cornovia in southern Cornouaille (*Kernev*) was named after the Cornish tribe of Cornovii. Poutrecoet was situated in the centre and Bro Erec'h accounted for the rest of southern Brittany including the inland area and the western part of the county of Vannes. These regions were ruled by different leaders from different families so that Brittany in effect was controlled by a collection of chiefs. These leaders were independent of each other on the whole but they sporadically banded together in order to raid into Frankish lands,

or to fend off a counter-attack. Thus the occasional ruler would
be pushed to the fore briefly such as Morvan and later Wihomarc.

The situation in eastern, or upper Brittany, was different. This
region had been more susceptible to Roman influences during the
Empire, and it held on to its Gallo–Roman identity while the west
was being Bretonized. The countryside here was more fertile and
the climate more favourable than that of the wet and windy west
and it was small wonder that the lands around the valley of the
Vilaine (*ar Gwilen*) were coveted by Breton and Frank alike.

After the fall of the Roman Empire the Franks created a new
order in north-west Europe. Under the leadership of Clovis at the
end of the fifth century they expanded their domain; this
culminated in the coronation of Charlemagne in 800. They
controlled a huge empire which included all the old Roman
provinces of Gaul, except Brittany. While the accepted boundary
was the river Vilaine the actual border between the Bretons and
Franks remained fluid throughout the early Middle Ages and
there was no sudden distinction between Breton and Frankish
Armorica. There was a zone of transition where population and
language mixed and merged; nevertheless it can be said that the
counties of Nantes and Rennes were (usually) Frankish lands,
and Frankish coins were minted there.

Raids from both sides of the border were common in the sixth
century. The Breton leader of Bro Erec'h, Waroc, was responsible
for attacking and occupying both Vannes and Nantes repeatedly
in the latter part of the century. The Frankish ruler Chilperic (and
his successor Guntramn) led the counter-attacks in order to regain
their territory. Nantes was a frequent target for Breton raiders
making off with the grape harvest.

During the seventh and early eighth century the contact
between Frankish rulers and Bretons seems to have become less
frequent. In 635 the Frankish ruler Dagobert I (622–38) decreed
that the Breton leader Judicaël should pay homage to him and the
leadership of the Frankish kings. Judicaël seems to have been a
typical warrior prince whose authority was based in Dumnonia.
He is described as the 'chief of Brittany and other lands' which
suggests that he may have conquered lands in the east also.

Whether his homage to Dagobert was an act of alliance or submission is not clear. Judicaël's reign however does seem to have been a time of peace and, if the absence of Frankish reports is anything to go by, the Bretons, apart from some occasional minor fighting, seem to have lived in comparable peace and isolation on the fringe of the Frankish domain until the middle of the eighth century. Our knowledge of this period stems from Frankish sources, so any in-fighting among Breton chiefs themselves has not been recorded for us.

The accession of Pippin III (the Short) to the Frankish throne in 751 saw the initiation of a more aggressive policy on the part of the Franks. Vannes was captured and it was incorporated, along with Nantes and Rennes, into the march of Brittany. This Frankish-held buffer zone was designed to withstand and contain the unruly Bretons to the west. Thus began a long period of raiding and suppression as the effectiveness of Frankish rule over this frontier area waxed and waned.

Breton unrest continued well into the ninth century and it was not curbed until the reign of Louis the Pious. Louis had to contend with the Breton leader Morvan whom he defeated and killed in 818. Another thorn in his side was Wihomarc who repeatedly broke his oath of loyalty in between bouts of insurrections. He was finally vanquished in 825. The Bretons were excellent horsemen and their light cavalry tactics meant that they could utilize the difficult terrain to their advantage. The brute force and burnt-earth tactics that the Carolingian Franks had used successfully in Saxony failed to break the Breton spirit.

Despite these difficulties Louis was determined to subdue the rebellious Bretons and incorporate them into his vision of a peaceful Christian empire under his leadership as Holy Roman Emperor. While campaigning in Brittany he had been horrified to discover to what extent Breton religious practices still reflected Celtic liturgical tradition. He immediately decreed that the revised rule of Saint Benedict should be imposed and applied to all Breton dioceses that were now re-attached to Tours. Thus he saw the Bretons as a moral threat as well as a military one.

Louis also had to attend to revolts within the Frankish aristocracy and one of his most rebellious barons held lands in the March of Brittany. This was Lambert, count of Nantes, against whom Louis brought out his entire army in 830. In the light of his problems in the frontier land, with recalcitrant Bretons and dissident Frankish noblemen, Louis decided to integrate Brittany into the empire by peaceful means. He appointed Nominoé as his *missus imperatoris in Britanniam*, or imperial agent in Brittany.

Who was Nominoé and why did Louis choose him to be his representative in Brittany? We know very little about Nominoé the man, other than he was almost certainly a native Breton. His own power base seems to have been centred on the Vannetais but Louis identified him as a leader who was able to unify the Bretons, at least in the frontier area. Breton rulers were really leaders of factions only; for example Wihomarc probably only held sway in northern Brittany. But as the Franks increased the pressure, more and more contingents were willing to band together under a single leader, albeit temporarily. Thus Nominoé succeeded in keeping the Bretons calm, after the unrest of 836–7, until the end of Louis' reign in 840.

Nominoé (also known as Nevenoe) has been hailed as a national hero by patriots, and nationalists have described him as the creator of the Breton nation. More recent historians have stripped away the more romantic view of him, but he remains important in popular tradition. In his anthology of ballads based on folk songs collected in the nineteenth century La Villemarqué claimed that Nominoé's exploits had remained in folk memory throughout the centuries and that one of the ballads he published in his *Barzaz Breiz* was a song of praise to the great man himself.

It was Nominoé's exploits after the death of Louis in 840 that caught later patriots' attention. His loyalty to the Frankish crown extended only to Louis himself and in the absence of a firm administrative network binding the Bretons into the Carolingian empire, once Louis was dead Nominoé felt no obligation whatsoever to his heir, Charles the Bald. Having initially sworn an oath of fidelity to Charles in 841, Nominoé then changed his tune in 843 and decided to ally himself with the rebel Lambert (probably the son of the Lambert mentioned above) who was anxious to regain the countship of Nantes for his family. With the help of the Bretons Nantes was attacked in 843 and the current count Rainald was killed. This battle failed to secure Nantes so a month later Lambert connived in a spectacular bloody assault by Vikings on the city during the feast of St John the Baptist on 24 June 843.

From the Nantes campaign onwards Nominoé continued to help Charles's enemies. He supported Lothar, Charles's eldest brother, Lambert and Pippin II of Aquitaine who all had interests in the area. Charles fought back and in 845 he made peace with Pippin and Lambert. But Nominoé was still an enemy and Charles and his army crossed the Vilaine in order to meet his foe at the battle of Ballon on 22 November 845. The battle was a spectacular defeat for Charles who had to escape to Le Mans.

In the summer of 846 Charles set out for Brittany again, but this time he did not come to fight but to make a formal peace with Nominoé. The defeat at Ballon had revealed the extreme fragility of royal power in north-west France. Nominoé had his own problems as the Vikings were becoming more active and there are hints that his own authority in Breton communities was being challenged. Thus Nominoé agreed to the terms which may have included Charles's recognition of Nominoé's right to rule the Bretons in return for acknowledgment of Charles's overlordship. This is the first occasion that a Breton leader was called 'dux' – duke.

Nominoé felt at the height of his powers. In May 849 he dismissed the five Breton bishops (of Alet, Dol, Quimper, Saint-Pol-de-Léon (*Kastell-Paol*) and Vannes) for simony (buying or selling ecclesiastical preferments, benefices etc.) and replaced them with his own nominees of his own race and language. These were not recognised by the pope or the Frankish church and were excommunicated. Nominoé's answer was to sack the cities of Rennes and Nantes and expel the Frankish bishop of Nantes replacing him also with his own nominee.

Lambert had helped Nominoé in the attack on Rennes and
Nantes and they went on to attack Le Mans also. The rebels
plundered and raided the Nantais and Anjou throughout the
winter of 850–1 dispersing the king's allies in the region. But
then Nominoé unexpectedly died in March 851 on Frankish
territory.

So was Nominoé the first true leader of the Breton nation? He
certainly developed from being a loyal royal agent in 830 to a
powerful ruler with expansionist policies after 843. The fact that
he could summon all the Breton bishops together and then
dismiss them is testimony to his power over the church in
Brittany. But there are signs that not all the Bretons felt bound to
him. Some seemed to wish to remain loyal to Charles after
Nominoé's defection in 843. And around 846 a Breton army
ignored the truce between Charles and Nominoé and attacked
Frankish lands. It is impossible to know how united the Bretons
were under Nominoé, or whether he had any sort of jurisdiction
over the far west which was far removed from Frankish raids and
influence. Nor did Nominoé and his family have the fiscal
prerogatives of rulership commonly reserved for early medieval
rulers or their appointed deputies, such as the right to strike coin,
to take the profits of justice or to collect tolls. Rather their
resources resembled those of the landowners in their own
entourage. It is also impossible to perceive Nominoé's incentives
or motives. We can assume, however, that his successful
plundering expeditions brought in booty which helped to build up
his own lordship over the Bretons.

Nominoé's sudden death on 7 March 851 raised Charles's
hopes that he could restore his claim over Brittany and in the
summer he launched an attack on the new Breton leader Érispoé,
Nominoé's son. However, after three days of bloody fighting,
Charles was defeated at Jengland-Beslé (*Besle*), on the left bank
of the Vilaine. This battle was even more humiliating than Ballon
and Charles barely escaped with his life. Érispoé agreed to peace
terms in return for the counties of Rennes, Nantes and the
'vicaria' of Retz (*Bro-Raez*) which was on the south bank of the
Loire. The Bretons now had access to the agricultural wealth of

the large rich estates of the east as well as the salt-panning industry and the viticulture of the Loire estuary. Mastery over the county of Retz meant access to ports on the south bank of the Loire and complete control of all shipping along this arterial waterway. Érispoé could now call himself 'prince of Brittany up to the Mayenne river'. He also received royal insignia from Charles and he was the first Breton to style himself as 'Érispoé – king.' Patriotic historiographical tradition, from at least the fourteenth century, claims that these grants meant that the Franks recognized Brittany as a fully independent kingdom, ruled by its own king and free from obligation to the French crown.

In 856 Érispoé's daughter was betrothed to Charles' eldest son, Louis the Stammerer, and Érispoé remained loyal to Charles until his own death in November 857.

Érispoé's successor and murderer was his cousin Salomon who embarked on a campaign to increase Brittany's lands even further. He allied his forces with west Frankish rebel magnates in 858. The rebels were not above hiring the services of Viking fleets on occasion, and the fighting continued until 863. Salomon and Charles then signed the treaty of Entrammes, and Charles recognized Salomon's claim to the lands that Érispoé had held, and added to them by granting him 'lands between the two waters', that is that part of western Anjou that lies between the Mayenne and Sarthe rivers. Salomon for his part recognized Frankish overlordship and swore fidelity to Charles.

The annual tributes were only paid twice however as in 865 Salomon joined forces with the Vikings again and raided Frankish lands in the Touraine region and up to Le Mans. In 867 Charles brought out his army but negotiations rather than a battle ensued and the treaty of Compiègne was signed. Charles annulled the homage and granted more lands to Salomon that included the Cotentin peninsula and the islands of Jersey and Guernsey. Salomon, not unreasonably, now called himself 'Prince of all Brittany and a big part of Gaul'. From now on Salomon remained on good terms with Charles and twice provided him with military aid against the Vikings.

Initially, like Nominoé, Salomon considered the church in
Brittany to be independent of the archbishopric of Tours and his
intention was to create a see at Dol. However, not all the
bishoprics over which he ruled supported Salomon's archie-
piscopal ambitions. The sees of Rennes and Nantes remained
Frankish in character and loyal to Tours and even the Breton see
of Alet never recognized Dol instead of Tours. Pope Nicholas
was vehemently opposed to the scheme, maintaining that
Brittany did not qualify for a new archbishopric and that there
was no evidence that there had ever been a see at Dol, despite
Breton claims to the contrary. By the pope's death in 867,
however, Salomon had made a lasting peace with Charles, and
the protesting bishops who had been deposed by Nominoé had
also died and the whole affair was allowed to gently fade away.

Salomon was the most successful and formidable of the Breton
rulers. By the time of his assassination in 874 he ruled over four
entire Frankish counties and parts of two others – Rennes,
Nantes, Avranches, Coutance, Pays de Retz and western Anjou.
His entourage was more extensive than Nominoé's humble court,
comprising up to fifty men at times and including bishops and
abbots. Throughout his reign Salomon's cortège remained almost
exclusively Breton and even when his court met in Frankish
territory its composition was almost entirely Breton. Militarily
Brittany was strong and eventually most of the lands that Charles
had granted on a temporary basis passed permanently into Breton
hands. Even the political turmoil that followed Salomon's death
was not enough to jeopardize Breton control of these Frankish
lands.

But Brittany was not a cohesive polity. There was no ethnic
identity based on a perceived common culture or origin to unite
all the people, on the contrary they were divided by language.
There was a certain geographical coherence in the sense that the
sea formed the frontier on three sides but the eastern boundary
was fluid and nebulous. In effect the cohesion and identity of the
principality was based on the personal lordship and private
wealth of the ruling family. By the end of Charles the Bald's
reign in 877 Brittany was a vast and powerful principality, and

although it was undeniably under Carolingian hegemony, in practice it was free from the day-to-day administrative rule of the West Frankish king.

As Brittany increasingly came into contact with its neighbour, Frankish influences began to penetrate Breton culture. Up until the middle of the ninth century Brittany's culture was more in tune with developments in Ireland and the British Isles than with France. The earliest extant Breton manuscripts are written in insular script and are almost indistinguishable from Old Welsh of the same date. Old Breton shared a common orthography with Old Cornish and Welsh until the eleventh century. Latin manuscripts were glossed in Irish as well as Breton, and there was a tendency to use Hisperic Latin, a highly ornate and rhetorical style associated with Ireland and Anglo-Saxon England. This was also the period of professional bards who probably sang eulogies at the courts of various chiefs, but, unlike in Wales, very little evidence of this has survived. The main centres of culture were the monasteries, especially Landévennec (*Landevenneg*), Léhon near Dinan, Alet and Redon. These each had a school, a scriptorium and a library. Artistically, a distinctive fantastic Celtic style was used in the miniatures that illustrated the manuscripts, especially the gospels. Saint Mark is represented by a horse's head, referring to the fact that his name, *marc'h* means horse in Breton. Saint John is portrayed with a bird's head and Saint Luke sometimes has four wings with a stylized human head. Only Mathew is human. Although these miniatures suggest insular prototypes, their effusiveness is wholly Breton and is largely unsurpassed by anything else in Europe of the same period.

This is also the period when *Buhez ar Sent*, the saints' lives, began to be written. These vividly record the founding of monasteries and churches by British saints. Many of these ninth-century lives included Irish story matter.

Many of the Breton monasteries were independent in character and Landévennec in particular was seen as distinctively Irish by ninth-century reformers. Major collections of Irish canonical material were transcribed there. It is worth mentioning that today, in the absence of a Breton national library, the most important collection of Breton manuscripts is kept at Landévennec abbey.

When the monastery of Saint-Sauveur de Redon was founded by Conwoion in 832 it became a centre for the dissemination of Carolingian ecclesiastical culture. Situated in the critical zone where Breton and Frank met it practised the revised Benedictine rule from the outset. Redon is of particular interest because of the survival of its cartulary, a huge collection of manuscripts that record the transactions and affairs of the monastery. As the abbey had lands in both Frankish and Breton Brittany, the manuscripts give us a glimpse of life on both sides and provide us with a unique insight into the period concerned.

The second half of the ninth century saw continental influences flowing into the region, and although the traditional orientation towards Ireland and Wales was in no way replaced, Breton intellectual life was appreciably different by the early tenth century. The Carolingian miniscule script was introduced, albeit intermingled with insular characters, and there was a revived interest in classical literature and Latin style. Under Louis's Benedictine reforms new links were forged with Frankish monasteries, opening up new routes for manuscripts to reach Brittany. Breton scholars became familiar with Virgil and other Latin poets, along with other Latin religious works and didactic texts like Priscian's grammar. Stimulated by both continental and insular sources Breton culture flowered and Breton hagiography in particular entered a golden age. While the Frankish influence may have had a profound effect, it should be remembered that it was the Breton elite that was affected; life at local village level would have been largely unchanged.

Salomon was the most powerful man in Brittany for seventeen years but in 874 a conspiracy against him brought his rule to an abrupt end. The plotters were Pascweten, Wrwhant and Wigo. Pascweten was the count of Vannes, a wealthy landowner with many estates and saltworks in south-eastern Brittany. He was a patron of Redon abbey, a prominent member in Érispoé and Salomon's retinue, and he was Salomon's son-in-law. Wrwhant's seigneurial interests lay in north-eastern Brittany.

The third member, Wigo son of Riwallon, was Salomon's nephew. Riwallon had been count of Cornouaille, a region which still had a strong sense of its own identity. Wigo's aim seems to have been the recovery of a certain amount of independence for Cornouaille, but Pascweten and Wrwhant were more ambitious, and after Salomon's death they fought each other for control of Brittany. By the middle of 876 both Pascweten and Wrwhant were dead and the dispute passed on to Alan, brother to Pascweten, and Judicaël, who was Érispoé's grandson. This dispute can be seen as a power struggle between the south-east of Brittany and the west. The western regions had grown resentful of domination by rulers based in the south-east. The supremacy continued, however, as Alan, who had inherited his brother's title of count of Vannes and had extensive interests in the county of Nantes, became the sole ruler when Judicaël, whose power base was in Cornouaille, died in 888 or 889.

Alan's main problem was the Vikings. From their base on the island of Noirmoutier (*Nervouster*) at the mouth of the Loire they had been raiding the south coasts and up the estuary causing havoc wherever they went for the previous forty years. Nantes was attacked in 843 and 868, the bishop of Vannes was captured in 854 and the community of Redon monastery had been forced inland by 866. The pirates were not one unified group however but several different bands and Breton rulers sometimes used them to their advantage, hiring their services as mercenaries, as Salomon did. Nevertheless the Bretons had had enough and under Alan's leadership they joined forces in order to push the Norse out and the result was the victorious battle of Questembert (*Kistreberzh*) in *c*.890. Alan's success in uniting the Breton aristocracy meant that the country was no longer a soft target and the Vikings went raiding elsewhere. Alan's reign of twenty years of peace earned him the title of Alan the Great.

After Alan's death in 908 his firm rule disintegrated and the country fell into disarray. Control of Nantes was lost and by 914 Fulk the Red, a Frankish vassal, was installed as count of Nantes. From his base there Fulk was able to recapture west Anjou for the Franks. In the north the Cotentin peninsula fell to the Normans.

In the county of Rennes a family of mixed Frankish and Breton origin, named Berengar, gained control. As the Franks clawed back the land they had lost, western Brittany was drawn into the orbit of the powerful West Saxon kings. Asser claims that there were Bretons amongst those who submitted to Alfred's lordship, although this claim only lasted one generation.

One reason that Breton leaders failed to keep control after 908 was that a full-scale universal attack was launched by the Vikings on the peninsula. Previously, the scattered Viking raids had been a problem mainly for the aristocracy and religious and proto-urban communities. Inland settlements had hardly been touched. The attacks were more likely to be on property than persons, and indeed, some of the Vikings were willing to be bought off while others became allies. Nevertheless, the Viking attacks of *c*.910–20 were much more violent and far-reaching, and by *c*.920 most of Brittany had been overrun. The social elite panicked and clergy and secular leaders alike fled. Whole monasteries decamped to safer parts of France, the monks of Landévennec venturing as far afield as Flanders to seek shelter. Even the more modest monks and priests departed as the Breton churches, stripped of their relics, were left unoccupied for years, perhaps even decades. There was no central leadership to coordinate resistance to the Norse, and such attempts had to be organized locally.

However, the Viking occupation of Brittany was short-lived. Alan the Great had a grandson, also called Alan, who proved to be worthy of his namesake. He had spent much of his youth in exile at court in Wessex and with his English godfather king Athelstan's help he mustered an army and attacked the Vikings at Dol, Plourivo (*Plourivoù*) and Nantes in 936–7. Thus Alan II reconquered Brittany and there is a dramatic description of him hacking his way through the brambles which had overgrown the town of Nantes. Although there was still the occasional Viking raid launched from the Seine valley in the 940s and again in 960, Brittany, in effect, had been cleared of the Vikings. The last recorded Viking raid on Brittany was in 1014–15.

Despite the empty churches, and deserted monasteries and manors, the Vikings had little lasting impact. There are very few Scandinavian place-names, even in the Loire valley, as evidence of the brief period of settlement. Life for ordinary people carried on much as before it seems. After 937 the monks returned to the lands they had always held and Alan II immediately revived Breton claims to Nantes and Rennes. There was one difference however; by the end of the tenth century there was a marked decrease in the use of the Breton language. During the ninth century Breton was the normal language of discourse throughout Breton Brittany, even in the south-east. It was also the language of authority in the Frankish east despite not being the language of the majority of the population there. Nominoé and Salomon promoted Breton, Salomon's retinue was always predominantly Breton and Breton was used, alongside Latin, for legal terms in the Redon cartulary. However, the period of exile meant that the aristocrats loosened their hold on their ethnic origins. By the time they returned they had been immersed in a milieu of late vulgar Latin and thereafter they increasingly turned to marriage with Franks. The monks had also been immersed in Frankish culture during exile. The upper classes thus ceased using Breton for communication and only in the west did the language remain prominent. Even there the upper social classes were fast being Gallicized and Breton was well on the way to being what it eventually became, a language spoken predominantly by illiterate peasants. The Viking occupation is probably only partly to blame for this. In all likelihood they speeded up a process that was going to happen anyway as Normandy, England and France became more powerful and hungry for domination.

3

Brittany becomes a duchy (936–1341)

The next 300 years saw Brittany develop into a country with permanent defined borders headed by a powerful duke who ruled with the aid of an efficient administrative system. The duke's progression from being an overlord only slightly richer and stronger than his peers around him, to powerful ruler whose authority was acknowledged throughout the peninsula, was a gradual one. Indeed, complete ducal power only truly became a reality when Brittany found itself under the control of an outside power, the king of England first of all, followed by the king of France.

This was also a time of ecclesiastical reform, monastic influxes and mass Christianization as the Breton church became completely assimilated into the mainstream Roman Catholic church, losing all trace of ancient Celtic practices. The country also experienced a demographic growth and the development of urban centres, although, compared to the rest of northern France, Brittany remained a predominantly rural society.

During this period we see the last Breton-speaking duke (Alan Fergant 1084–1119) as the upper classes proceeded to abandon the language altogether. The language frontier continued its shift westwards, although there is evidence that Breton was still spoken in Saint-Brieuc in the early thirteenth century. Conversely this period also saw the British legend of King Arthur and his knights gain huge popularity as the stories of the 'matter of Britain' caught the imagination of north-west Europe. This material, popularized by Geoffrey of Monmouth, was probably partly based on Breton oral traditions. The forest of Brocéliande (*Breselien*), where Merlin and Vivienne had their encounters, became a revered place, and one French chronicler wrote in the twelfth century that if a traveller were to go to Brittany and proclaim in a village square that Arthur was dead, he would probably be lynched. It is significant therefore that when it happened that the heir to the duchy was a new-born baby, and thus a time of great insecurity and concern for the future, his widowed mother named him Arthur.

When Alan II (936–52) crossed over from England to Brittany to claim his inheritance in 936 he not only had to flush out the Vikings and accept the loss of the lands in Cotentin and Avranches, he also had the Breton barons to contend with. These were a class of men who continued to cause difficulties to his successors for years to come. As was the case in neighbouring provinces, Brittany was slowly developing into a feudal society as seigneurial families increased in number and in wealth. These powerful landlords built castles and had their own private armies and by the late twelfth century Brittany was divided into about forty major castellanies. Some of them were descended from minor officials who over the years had built up a local power base, while others had taken advantage of the flight of the monks to add church lands to their own. They were men like Hervé de Léon, Raoul de Fougères and Eudon de Porhöet, men who would not allow a duke to rule over them with impunity. They valued their independence, and any infringement on their privileges, as they saw it, was fiercely resisted.

Initially the duke of Brittany was simply one powerful lord amongst other powerful lords and it was not clear at the outset which of the most prominent dynasties would prevail. The position of duke oscillated between the families of Rennes and Nantes, each being reluctant to acknowledge the other's superiority when they had the upper hand. The house of Cornouaille also joined the contenders at a later date. The way towards a legitimate heir for Brittany was not straightforward. Even when all the lands and titles of the three main families fell into the hands of one man in 1066, Hoël proved to be such a weak and ineffectual leader that the position of duke was seriously undermined and the barons rose up once again.

Hoël's son Alan IV (1084–1119) was more successful in uniting the three dynasties. Leaving Nantes safe in his brother's hands Alan seized the city of Rennes, imprisoning his recalcitrant great-uncle Geoffrey Grenonat. This act ensured the support of the remainder of the Rennais barons. Despite this success the duke's power did not extend further north where the powerful barons of Penthièvre (*Pentevr*) and Trègor (*Bro-Dreger*) refused to accept his supremacy over them. However, nor did they refute his authority over the rest of Brittany and thus an internal peace was established during Alan's reign. He was given the epithet Fergant, meaning 'brave' or 'perfect'.

The other problem that the Breton dukes had to contend with were the powerful rulers of neighbouring territories. By the mid-ninth century the mighty Carolingian Frankish dynasty had been replaced by the Capetian family who, initially at least, had much less control over the regions. So although they were ostensibly still vassals to the king of France, the Breton dukes did not have to take him into account the way that Nominoé, Salomon and Érispoé had to. Rather, they were much more concerned with the ambitions of the duke of Normandy and the counts of Blois and Anjou. Whenever the marcher barons revolted Brittany's frontiers were endangered as the Franks welcomed any opportunity to encroach on Brittany's territory. Various Breton dukes tried to stave off intervention by entering into marriage alliances with their covetous neighbours. Thus Geoffrey I (992–1008) married Havoise, the sister of the duke of Normandy and Alan III (1008–40) married Berthe from the house of Blois. The death of Alan Fergant's first wife, Constance, daughter of the duke of Normandy, gave Alan the opportunity to forge an alternative alliance when he remarried, taking Ermengarde, the daughter of the count of Anjou, as his second wife. In fact, Brittany's frontiers were consolidated from the beginning of the eleventh century as it was generally accepted that the former Frankish lands of Nantes and Rennes were now firmly within the duchy.

One of Brittany's most powerful neighbours during this period was William, duke of Normandy, who proceeded to conquer England and establish an Anglo-Norman dynasty there. But before embarking for England he had an encounter with the Breton duke Conan II (1040–66). His exploits in Brittany are the subject of the first scenes of the Bayeux tapestry.

Conan II had more than one internal insurgency to quell and he found himself surrounded by rebellious aristocrats. He tried to gain control of Nantes and Cornouaille, causing a minor civil war which only ended in 1054 with his defeat. Ten years later, in 1064, one of the barons within his own demesne of Rennes rose up against him. Rivallon possessed the castles of Dol and Combourg (*Komborn*) that guarded the frontier with Normandy. When Conan attacked the fortress at Dol, in response to his insubordination, Rivallon turned to the duke of Normandy for assistance. What should have been another minor rebellion for Conan turned out to be a major incident as William (the Conqueror to be) charged over the border with his army, liberated Dol, captured the fortress of Dinan and chased Conan all the way to Rennes. The Bayeux tapestry portrays Conan as a coward secretly descending the city walls of Dol by rope in order to flee from his Norman conqueror. Be that as it may, William failed to consolidate his achievements in Brittany, facing too many problems with maintaining supply lines and fending off persistent brigands. Thus William withdrew, leaving Conan to finally crush the disloyal Rivallon.

As long as Normandy, Blois and Anjou were at loggerheads with each other, Brittany could attempt to play one off against each other and gain a breathing space. But as soon as Normandy and Anjou forged an alliance, as they did in 1127, Brittany's days as an independent duchy were numbered. The beginning of the end came in 1148 when Conan III decided to disinherit his son and leave the duchy in the hands of his grandson who was still a baby. During his last days Conan arranged for his son-in-law Eudon de Porhöet to be in charge of the duchy while waiting for the little Conan to grow up. The next fifteen years passed by with relative calm for Brittany: Eudon was popular with the barons and Normandy was much too embroiled in problems of succession to bother about Brittany. However, when the time came for Conan IV to succeed to the duchy, Eudon was unwilling to give up his power. Conan fled to England where he was welcomed at court. There he appealed for assistance to gain his rightful inheritance, but in doing so he was paving the way for

Brittany to gain a new master. The king of England in 1154 was Henry II who was not only the duke of Normandy but count of Anjou, Touraine, Maine and Aquitaine also. It was inevitable that such a powerful and forceful man as Henry would leap at the opportunity to control Brittany as well. He backed Conan with military support, allowing him to win back the duchy in 1156, but he intervened directly ten years later when Conan proved to be ineffectual in quashing a rebellion. The barons had risen up again and did so in their usual chaotic and disorderly manner and it was easy for Henry's military machine to crush them when he came to the peninsula in 1166. In the light of this easy victory Henry came to the conclusion that Conan was either unable or unwilling to control the barons and Henry forced him to abdicate as duke. To be fair to Conan, his apparent incompetence may have been more of a respect for local customs as he sought to appease the barons in a more conciliatory fashion. Either way, it is reasonable to suppose that Henry was waiting for an excuse to intercede and assume control.

Brittany was now controlled directly by Henry and he continued the task of suppressing any form of revolt. He was overbearing and authoritarian in the extreme and succeeded in completely subduing the barons with his superior military strength and ruthlessness, although it took even him thirteen years to do so. He also laid down the foundation of an effective administrative system. He divided the country into eight administrative regions (possibly developing an existing structure) and appointed a seneschal to each one. These men were personally appointed and trusted by Henry and they were responsible for the day-to-day running of each region, fulfilling such duties as issuing writs and administering justice.

Henry arranged for his young son Geoffrey to be betrothed to the even younger Constance, daughter of Conan, and when Geoffrey was deemed old enough to marry her in 1181, Henry handed over the government of Brittany to him.

Geoffrey was much more popular than his autocratic father. He acted independently, choosing his own men to be officials and this was appreciated by the barons who did not rebel during his short reign. Lesser men also benefited as Brittany was now at peace and prospered as they no longer had to worry about enemies. The Loire river in particular was able to develop as a safe major trade route. The administrative framework established by Henry began to function properly under Geoffrey. The first ducal legal text, the Assizes of Geoffrey, was produced in 1186. This established the practice of primogeniture, thus effectively preventing the piecemealing of fiefdoms from generation to generation. Ducal influence now reached all parts of the peninsula as even the furthest remotest western regions had been added to the ducal demesne, as one by one the lands of the disloyal barons were confiscated. Geoffrey might well have founded a new and successful dynasty for Brittany with Constance had he not died prematurely in 1186.

The duchy of Brittany now lay in duchess Constance's hands, and she gave birth to Arthur in 1187, a few months after Geoffrey's death. The young widow ruled efficiently with the support of the barons although Henry kept a close eye on her, ensuring her loyalty by forcing her to marry Ranulf de Chester, a powerful Norman baron who also had lands in England. Ranulf proved to be very much the absent husband and Constance seems to have governed quite effectively with the aid of her seneschals. When Arthur was eight and a half Constance summoned the most powerful barons to Rennes and there declared that Arthur was the rightful duke of Brittany. This act of Breton self-determination incensed the Anglo-Norman king Richard the Lionheart (his father Henry II had died in 1189) and he proved to be as autocratic as his father. He effected the kidnapping of Constance by her own husband Ranulf and then sent over a pillaging army to teach the Bretons a lesson. Little Arthur was able to flee in time and he took refuge with the king of France in Paris. King Philip Augustus had been good friends with Geoffrey, but his protection of Arthur only lasted until 1198 when the young duke found himself entrusted to his uncle Richard's care. Constance was released on condition that she succumbed to Richard henceforth.

In 1199 Richard was killed, leaving the throne to his youngest brother. This was king John I (1199–1216) and he was accepted as sovereign indisputably in England, Normandy and Aquitaine. However, feudal practice in Anjou, Maine and Touraine dictated that in the absence of a direct heir it was the oldest brother of the dead king who should take precedence and, if he were dead, then it was his heir who was considered to be next in line. Richard the Lionheart was the second son of Henry II, Geoffrey the third and John the fourth. Thus, according to this principle, Arthur of Brittany, being the son of Geoffrey, was the rightful heir to the throne. The great Angevine empire of the Plantagenet family was in danger of collapse.

Meanwhile, the king of France decided to intervene. Philip Augustus had previously protected Arthur but had then been distracted by other major problems; these had now been solved and the Capetian king was eager to exploit a situation that could ruin the powerful Plantagenets. He supported the annulment of Constance's marriage and encouraged her to marry Guy de Thouars who was a Poitevin lord loyal to the Capetians. Philip also sent troops to aid Arthur in his battles in Touraine. The Bretons gratefully received the French king's patronage, regarding him as the saviour of the young duke. In reality they were seeing the beginning of a process that would provide Brittany with yet another master.

In 1200 Philip and John signed the treaty of Vernon which granted the guardianship of Arthur to Philip, but which also conceded that Arthur should pay homage to John on behalf of Brittany, on the grounds that John was duke of Normandy and as such overlord of Brittany. Arthur was also to relinquish his claims to Anjou, Touraine and Maine.

Nevertheless, in 1202, hostilities broke out again between the kings of England and France. Philip Augustus, as the suzerain of France, confiscated all of John's continental possessions. Brittany, Anjou, Maine and Touraine he gave to Arthur, who had recently paid homage to the French king at Gournay. Fighting ensued and John himself crossed the channel to join the battle for his inheritance. On 31 July 1202 John's forces captured and imprisoned his nephew Arthur during the siege of Mirabeau, in Poitou. Arthur was moved to Rouen where he was assassinated, on John's orders, in April 1203. He was aged sixteen.

The anxious barons and bishops of Brittany convened in Vannes at the end of 1203 to discuss their precarious future. Duchess Constance had died two years earlier and their only hope was her third husband, Guy de Thouars. They declared their loyalty to him and announced that Alice, his daughter by Constance, was now the sole legitimate heir to the duchy of Brittany. Meanwhile the fighting continued, with Rennes suffering the full brunt of John's soldiers who also set fire to the cathedral at Dol. Nevertheless, Normandy fell to Philip and his allied forces in 1204, and Guy de Thouars played his part, capturing Mont-Saint-Michel, Pontorson and Avranches. He even got as far as Caen.

Philip himself ruled Brittany in 1206 when he appeared in person briefly at Nantes and coins were minted in his name. A year later, he handed over the reins to Guy de Thouars. In 1212 he intervened directly when he decided that Alice should marry Pierre de Dreux, a French Capetian prince who was great grandson to Louis VI. They were married in December 1213, he was twenty-three, she was thirteen.

Pierre de Dreux was only meant to govern Brittany until an eventual heir would be born and attain majority. In the event he ruled for twenty-three years and left quite a mark on the duchy. One of his first acts was to attack the excessive powers of the upper echelons of the church. This is probably what earned him the nickname of Pierre Mauclerc (enemy of the clergy). Pierre was not anti-religious or anti-clerical even, but rather he was simply attempting to enforce the strict policies of his master Philip Augustus. In 1218 Pierre was excommunicated by the bishop of Nantes who felt that he had gone too far when he attempted to impose a tax on the city that the bishop felt was his own realm. In 1225 Pierre launched an attack on the church's tribunals that were rivalling the ducal tribunals. Another source of frustration to Pierre was that most of the episcopal cities were episcopal domains which meant that the duke had no control over their financial or military affairs, and this he sought to change. He also attacked abuses such as the levy placed on the faithful for weddings and funerals. Some of Pierre's lay subjects followed his example, refusing to pay death duties and confiscating tithes. In 1228 Pope Gregory IX excommunicated Pierre imposing an interdict on Brittany that meant that the only sacraments allowed were baptism and extreme unction. This did not deter Pierre in 1234 from claiming the revenues of the bishopric of Nantes when that position became vacant. The quarrel with the church did not come to an end until 1236 when Pierre went on a crusade.

Pierre also increased ducal control over his lay vassals. He restricted castle building, insisted on precise military obligations and acquired the lands of barons who died with no grown-up heirs. He also tried to limit local customs such as the right to profit from shipwrecks. These measures seemed perfectly reasonable to a feudal lord from the Ile-de-France but he met with fierce resistance from the Breton aristocracy. Despite their protests Pierre's defeat of lord Amaury de Craon in 1223 at Châteaubriant (*Kastell-Briant*) made him the indisputable master of Brittany.

Until 1223 Pierre de Dreux was absolutely loyal to the French crown. However, the death of Philip Augustus weakened the French monarchy considerably, Louis VIII only lasted three years and he was followed by the regency of Blanche de Castille. Pierre felt no loyalty to the new sovereign and in 1226 he plotted with other great vassals at Avignon, and established friendly relations with England, now ruled by Henry III. On 9 October 1226 they signed a pact which decreed that should Pierre and Alice's son Jean die prematurely, then the duchy of Brittany would go to Henry. In 1229 Pierre's defiance of the king of France developed into a full-scale war on Brittany's frontiers. The hostilities continued for five years until Pierre was finally forced to surrender in 1234. Three years later he yielded the duchy to his son Jean, and departed on a crusade to Egypt. He died in 1250.

Jean I (1237–86) was altogether a more peaceable character than his colourful father. He was prudent, economical and did not care for adventure, he willingly paid homage to the king of

France on his accession to the duchy. Jean continued his father's policy of suppressing the barons and he proved to be even more efficient at it. Jean's way was to ruin the noblemen financially while appealing to their vanity. His favourite method was to encourage the barons to overspend by lending them considerable amounts of money. When the day came to pay him back and they found that they could not afford to do so, Jean would confiscate their land. In this way the lands of the ducal demesne increased as Jean acquired the estates of Gourin, Hennebont (*an Henbont*) and Dinan to name but a few. Jean I's reign lasted half a century and his contribution to Brittany was fifty years of peace and full coffers. In fact Jean I's three successors, Jean II (1286–1305), Arthur II (1305–12) and Jean III (1312–41) also avoided war and disputes and Brittany experienced an unprecedented period of peace that lasted more than a century.

Jean I and his successors were absolute in their loyalty to the French throne. They participated in Capetian exploits in Flanders in 1297, 1314, and 1328, raised taxes for this war in 1303 and implemented the measures against the Knight Templars in 1308. The bonds were tightened even further in 1297 when the Breton dukes were promoted to the status of peer of France. This was an honour shared by only a handful of other feudal noblemen and it cemented Brittany's loyalty to the Capetians.

The French kings began to interfere in the day-to-day running of Brittany, ensuring that any ducal prerogatives would not be detrimental to superior royal authority. For example, royal bailiffs and senechals active in frontier regions would encourage Bretons to use the king's tribunal appeal system rather than that of the duke's. Another way that the French king, Saint Louis in this case, demonstrated his supremacy was by the imposition of his own coinage on Brittany and other great fiefdoms while forbidding the circulation of his vassal's coins within the royal demesne.

Yet the royal enthusiasm for increased centralization of powers was also to the advantage of the duke as he benefited from a more efficient and comprehensive administrative system. Precise procedures were established and followed and now a chamberlain took care of the duchy's finances and a marshall looked after the army. The essential unit was the council, which was composed of the members of a small number of families; but when important decisions had to be made, bishops, canons, barons and the most important officials came together to form a full *parlement*.

Despite the peace and prosperity, urban growth in Brittany was relatively slow compared to the rest of northern France, and the towns remained under the control of the seigneurial lords. Out of the sixty or so towns that had sprung up during the thirteenth century, twenty-eight were dependant on the local baron, fifteen were ducal towns, and five were episcopal fiefdoms. One belonged to Redon monastery and the remainder were divided between several urban lords. Not one of these towns had a municipal council or some sort of administrative independence. Commercial and craft developments, which are often associated with an urban bourgeoisie, in Brittany remained close to rural activities with artisans combining their profession with agriculture of some sort.

One interesting exception is that of Saint-Malo (*Sant-Maloù*), whose inhabitants are known for their independent spirit. In 1308 this sea port rebelled against its local ruler, the bishop, and in his place formed a sort of communal government. The town had a mayor, jurors, a general assembly, archives, a seal and a meeting place. Unfortunately this interesting experiment was quashed very quickly by royal intervention and the episcopal governance was reimposed.

Saint-Malo was a port that took advantage of its position at the heart of the Angevine empire, other towns developed around castles like those at Josselin (*Josilin*) and Fougères (*Felger*), others appeared where the ria was bridgeable as at Hennebont and Landerneau. Marcher towns like Vitré offered protection in a dangerous area, and some interior towns like Montfort (*Moñforzh*) and Quintin (*Kintin*) represent the colonization of the forest and the development of new agricultural land, sorely needed at this time of population expansion. Only two medieval Breton towns seem to have been deliberately planned with a gridiron of streets, that of Saint-Aubin-du-Cormier (*Sant-Albin-an-Hiliber*) and Gavres (*Gavr*), both founded by Pierre de Dreux. The major centres in Brittany were Nantes and Rennes that had populations of about 13,000 or 14,000 by the fifteenth century (this is the earliest that any figure can be calculated reasonably accurately), followed by Dinan, Fougères and Vannes that probably had only 5,000 inhabitants each. Otherwise Brittany was predominantly rural, a landscape of dispersed habitations, scattered farms and hamlets and a plethora of small towns.

Some urban development, such as that of Dol and Saint-Pol-de-Léon, evolved around important religious centres and this was another area that developed during this period in Brittany's history, the expansion of the monasteries. During the twelfth century thirteen new monasteries were founded by the Cistercians in Brittany, accompanied by ten Augustinian establishments and three further native Benedictine foundations. The Hospitalliers and Templars also came to Brittany to spread their way of life. There were new houses, supplementing the original native foundations like Landévennec and Redon, which were re-established after the departure of the Vikings. The monasteries contributed to the social and economic development of Brittany, and coming from outside as most of them did, helped reinforce ties with France in a cultural and economic sense.

The so-called Gregorian reforms were beginning to take effect throughout the country also. The family dynasties of bishops had largely disappeared by the early twelfth century but canons and parish priests still needed reforming in this matter. Tithes and other ecclesiastical property that had been stolen by lay noblemen were now returned to the church, although more often than not it was the local monastery who received it rather than the secular church. In this way the monks found themselves responsible for much parochial work in later medieval Brittany. Superstition and unorthodox practices were still abroad and the reformers struggled to educate the masses in mainstream conventional Christianity. Pagan and agrarian rites were slowly absorbed with crosses, shrines, and chapels strategically placed next to venerated wells and stones. The fertility cult parades and the ritual circuits that followed the sun's path were metamorphosized into *pardons* and Christian processions.

The Breton church was completely absorbed into the French church by now. In 1199 Pope Innocent III proclaimed his definite preference for Tours as the metropole of the ecclesiastical province and Dol's claim to be an archbishopric was now obliterated for ever. The Breton church as a separate entity with its own administration had completely disappeared by the thirteenth century.

Brittany's century of peace was to come to an end in 1341. While the Capetian/Valois and the Plantagenets were heading towards the Hundred Years War (1337–1453), a sterile and ineffective duke in Brittany was preparing the way for civil war.

4

The War of Succession and the end of the duchy (1341–1532)

Brittany's war of succession (1341–64), which pitted Breton against Breton, did not prevent the country from developing administrative institutions appropriate for an emerging state during the fourteenth century and the relative calm of the following years provided the dukes of Montfort with the means to extend and reinforce those institutions. Nevertheless, Brittany's recurring inability to produce a male heir to the ducal throne impeded its potential of becoming a fully-fledged state and instead this only accelerated the process of absorption by its powerful and covetous neighbour, France.

After the childless duke Jean III's death in 1341, there was doubt as to who would inherit his position. He had refused to designate a successor so there were two contenders, his half-brother Jean de Montfort, and Charles de Blois nephew to the king of France who was married to Jean III's niece, Jeanne de Penthièvre. Both men received succour and military aid from outside powers, namely France and England, and thus the Hundred Years War, which had erupted a few years previously, now opened up a new front on the soil of Brittany.

Both pretenders had supporters in Brittany. Charles de Blois, backed by the French, had followers who included the majority of the grand aristocracy and high churchmen, most of whom possessed lands in France. He enjoyed support amongst the bourgeoisie of Upper Brittany, especially around Rennes, where they were engaged in commercial links with France. The lesser noblemen, on the other hand, which included the esquires and knights, adhered to Jean de Montfort and his English sponsors. This was the class that had most benefited from holding ducal offices and they suspected that their position would be undermined by too close an association with an increasingly centralizing French monarchy. The ports along Brittany's long and rugged coastline also favoured the Montfort cause as they had close maritime links with England.

The two sides clashed for the first time in Nantes in 1341 where Jean had established his stronghold. But the French troops succeeded in blockading the city port, forcing it to surrender on 18 November. Jean de Montfort was captured and imprisoned.

Jean's cause was now taken up by his wife Jeanne de Flandres. The Breton war of succession is sometimes referred to as the 'war of the two Jeannes' as both Jeanne de Flandres and Jeanne de Penthièvre were strong-willed women, absolutely committed to fighting for possession of the duchy. While Montfort himself might have accepted a generous compensation in return for renouncing his claim, Jeanne de Flandres was determined to win the duchy for her son. Jeanne de Penthièvre, likewise, was adamant that the duchy was her rightful inheritance. She was the driving force behind Charles de Blois who would much rather have been a Franciscan monk than a fighting duke. He had no military qualities whatsoever, his health was fragile and his intensely religious lifestyle led him to be venerated during his lifetime.

Jeanne de Flandres negotiated a formal alliance with England in the following February of 1342, having rallied Montfort's wavering supporters in Vannes and around the south and west of the country, taking her young son Jean with her, showing him off to boost morale. She recognized the English king Edward III as the rightful king of France and English troops now arrived on Brittany's shores. There followed several battles and the Montfort camp succeeded in winning a chain of fortresses all along the coast, from Morlaix in the north to Guérande (*Gwenrann*) at the mouth of the Loire.

Edward III himself arrived in Brittany and indeed came face to face with the king of France, Philip VI, at Malestroit (*Malastred*) in January 1343. Rather than fighting however they signed a truce and Edward III returned to England taking Jeanne de Flandres and her two young sons with him. Montfort was released by Philip VI on condition that he was not to return to Brittany.

The fighting continued with Blois slowly gaining ground but in 1345 Montfort broke the condition of his release and landed at Brest at the head of an English army. In June 1345 he defeated Blois at the battle of la Lande-Cadoret, north of Josselin, but he himself died soon after, leaving a five-year-old son in the Tower of London as his heir. In 1347 Charles de Blois was captured at the battle of La Roche-Derrien (*Ar Roc'h Derrien*) and he joined the young Jean de Montfort in the Tower.

The war dragged on for another eighteen years, although food shortages and plague epidemics meant that much of the fighting was disorganized skirmishes and there were not many major incidents other than the battle of Mauron (*Maoron*) 1352 and the siege of Rennes 1356–7, one of the longest of the Hundred Years War. The Anglo–Breton camp was victorious in both cases.

In 1362 Edward III agreed that the young Jean de Montfort, now aged twenty-two, should return to Brittany and the administration of Brittany was officially handed over to him in July of that year. Nevertheless the question of succession was not finally resolved until 1364 with the death of Blois (who had been freed in 1356 on payment of a vast ransom) at the battle of Auray (*Alre*). Jeanne de Penthièvre finally gave up and the king of France, Charles V by now, recognized Jean de Montfort as having won the duchy. The treaty of Guérande, signed in 1365, recognized Montfort as duke Jean IV who must pay homage to the king of France. Jeanne de Penthièvre was allowed to keep the lands she had inherited directly from her father and the title of duchess until her death.

However the new duke was not popular with Breton high aristocracy. Having got used to acting independently during the long period of anarchy, the barons found Jean IV authoritarian in his effort to control them. The disaffected ones collected around one Olivier de Clisson, a lord who hated the English with venom and who had close family ties with the Penthièvre house: his daughter had married Jeanne de Penthièvre's son.

When war between France and England broke out again in 1369 duke Jean IV, despite being a vassal to the king of France, entered into secret negotiations with the English. When 4,000

English troops were permitted to land at Saint-Malo in 1372 the Breton nobility seized the opportunity to get rid of the duke by appealing to the king of France. Charles V responded to his disobedient vassal's actions by sending the highly talented general Du Guesclin to occupy the peninsula in 1373. Duke Jean IV had to flee back to England.

The duchy was now administered, in the name of the king of France, by the duke of Anjou, Olivier de Clisson and the viscount de Rohan. As Jean IV continued to be disloyal to Charles V this would have been a good time for the French king to confiscate Brittany altogether. A decision made at the *parlement* of Paris and a court of peers intended to do just that, but the king faced an obstacle, the Bretons themselves. Having realized that the king of France would be a much more formidable, demanding and effective overlord than any duke could be, and seeing their rights and privileges about to be quashed by absorption into France, a number of the noblemen of Brittany, mostly the great lords of the eastern counties, signed an act of association in 1379 that opposed any unity with the kingdom of France. They then begged Jean IV to return. This he did, having first sworn loyalty to Richard II of England, and he landed at Saint-Servan soon after. The return of Jean IV meant the return of war as the king of France sent troops under Bertrand du Guesclin once more to fight the Breton duke, but this time he was unsuccessful.

Thus Jean IV could rule as duke once more and Charles V's death in 1380, the following year, enabled a reconciliation between the two sides and legal relations with France were re-established. This was to the relief of many Breton noblemen who were uneasy with the idea of France as an out-and-out enemy as so many of the greater ones had lands in France. The second treaty of Guérande was signed in April 1381. Jean IV paid homage to the French throne (now occupied by a minor, Charles VI), paid a fine and sent his English councillors and soldiers back home. The king of England confiscated the county of Richmond (which had been given to Jean IV's father by Edward III) in retaliation, but Jean IV was astute enough to realize that friendship with France was now the more sensible option. The duchy was henceforth firmly in the hands of a Montfort duke, as it would be for the next hundred years.

The response of Jean IV's son, Jean V (1399–1442) to the question of loyalty to France and friendship with England was to attempt a strictly neutral position. He kept up a cordial relationship with England, signing various truces, taking measures to suppress piracy and giving licences to Bretons to supply the English troops in Normandy. Jean V even supported the duke of Bedford who was ruling northern France in the name of king Henry VI. Yet he still fulfilled his vassal duties to France, taking care that they would not clash with English interests. This is why he sent troops to fight at Agincourt in 1415, but made certain that he personally arrived too late to take any part in the battle. This policy of strict neutrality succeeded in keeping Brittany out of the Hundred Years War which was still raging.

Jean V's successors found it more prudent to have a Francophile attitude as they sensed that the tide was turning against England. His two sons François I (1442–50) and Pierre II (1450–7) and his brother who succeeded them as duke Arthur III (1457–8) all participated personally in campaigns against England.

During the reign of the Montfort dukes Brittany experienced a period of relative calm that allowed the administrative infrastructure of the duchy to be consolidated. Brittany now had a general council of ten to twenty members, many of whom were lawyers, and it was this body of men who advised the duke on matters of governance. They were very powerful, and competent and wise councillors could make up for any duke that was weak or incapable and still ensure that the country was governed effectively. The council was chaired by the chancellor, and he represented the duke in his absence.

The chancellor was also responsible for the chancery that drafted and dispatched ducal acts. The chancery clerks, whose numbers increased from about eight in 1400 to twenty-four in 1488, recorded the most important decisions on elegant parchments tied with swathes of green and red silk and sealed with green wax.

The chamber of accounts was based on the model of the English exchequer and the French *chambres de comptes*. Its main area of concern was the revenue from taxes, and the management of the duchy's finances developed to such an extent that by the late fifteenth century there were more than 400 officials involved.

When the duke needed to impose extra or new taxes he assembled the estates, and in fact these representatives of the people met up about once a year. The Breton estates were made up of three parts and as well as taxes they also discussed important issues that affected the duchy. The first estate comprised about a hundred noblemen, the second estate consisted of about sixty bishops and prelates (only the higher echelons of the church were allowed in) and the third estate was made up of about thirty members of the bourgeoisie who represented some twenty-five towns. Consulting the estates was a way for the duke to keep in touch with his people and listen to their concerns and demands, although, as the make up of the body shows, the people as far as he was concerned meant the rich and important rather than the mostly rural masses.

In 1485 a high court of justice, called a *parlement*, was established. This institution consisted of fifteen or so magistrates and acted as an appeal court as it dealt with cases from the lower ducal courts and seigneurial tribunals.

Thus Brittany had most of the trappings of a medieval state and in this sense it was quite typical of many other European states of the time; but it still had no capital. The chamber of accounts was based at Vannes, where the *parlement* also met, but the chancery's archives were located in Nantes, and the crowning of the duke took place at Rennes. The estates would meet almost anywhere, and the council followed the duke as he shared his time between his favourite residences, which included Vannes and Nantes but also Auray, Suscinio (*Susinioù*) and Dinan. François II (1458–88) preferred to keep his court at Nantes, and this afforded some stability to the council at least. What is noticeable about this multi-located administration however is that, with the exception of Vannes, it is largely based in the east, in Upper Brittany. Very rarely did the estates or the duke venture further west than Vannes, and most of the councillors and state officials were also from the French-speaking east.

Despite these state institutions, the dukes and their entourages were acutely aware of Brittany's inferior position vis-à-vis France and the chief councillors were ever vigilant in guarding against any royal infringement on the duke's position and prerogatives. They always attended homage ceremonies and meetings with royal advisors armed with reams of documents proving the legality of the duke's status. They also ensured during the various homage ceremonies that took place that the duke's rank as vassal appeared to be largely symbolic as they insisted that he took the oath standing rather than kneeling, and armed with a sword.

With a comprehensive system of governance now in place the duke's position within his own duchy was a powerful one. He alone had the authority to raise troops and levy taxes, and not even the most powerful nobleman was allowed to build a castle without the duke's permission. The last great fiefdom which could have posed any threat to the duke was Penthièvre and François II eliminated this anomaly by confiscating the lands in 1465. The dukes also consolidated their position by living the lifestyle appropriate to a powerful medieval duke. Castle building, lavish entertainment at court and elaborate ceremonies were all designed to impress. The numerous banquets, tournaments and hunts were all opportunities for the duke to visibly display his wealth and enhance his image. Jean IV in particular loved breeding fine hunting dogs that were sometimes presented as a token of ducal esteem. Other manifestations of the duke's eminence was the coronation ritual, revised in 1403 especially for Jean V so that it would be even more impressive, and the duchy's coins, cast with the likeness of the crowned duke. Another mark of a sovereign prince was an order of knights; so for example the Order of the Ermine was established in 1379 to commemorate those who had fallen at Auray in 1364.

Although this lavish lifestyle was politically necessary it did mean that for much of the time the duchy was living beyond its means. The loss of the Richmond lands in England had affected the duke's revenues considerably, and Brittany's economy was still relatively under-developed.

This is not to say that the Breton economy was stagnant, there was some real progress between 1380 and 1470, and although growth was then hampered by the political troubles, it picked up again in 1500. However, Brittany's prosperity, as the spate of new and reconstructed castles, cathedrals and manor houses in the Gothic style testify, even in the good times of Jean V, François I and Pierre II, was relative.

Agricultural developments included the expansion of stock rearing in the east, and the increased use of water and windmills. Serfdom was finally abolished in 1486 by François II. Crop yields were low compared to more advanced regions and the years 1447–68, with a succession of floods and excessive rain, followed by a series of hailstorms, and finally a period of drought, were difficult times indeed for the rural population in particular.

The sea began to be exploited more than ever during this period and wherever a boat could land there seemed to be a fishing community. For many families it was a useful way of supplementing the meagre income got from agriculture. Several small new ports emerged, such as Audierne (*Gwaien*), Concarneau (*Konk-Kerne*) and Morlaix, and it is estimated that there were at least 2,000 Breton boats in existence at this time. Breton sailors and merchants continued to trade along the traditional routes up the Loire river, across the Channel to England, and down the coast of France to Portugal and Galicia. New avenues were barred to them however as the Hanseatic League and the Dutch controlled the Baltic sea. Neither did Breton merchants succeed in the Mediterranean, despite the immense importance of this inland sea to trade in general in the middle ages. The trade also suffered from piracy, and once the Hundred Years War was over unfavourable competition increased as the duchy could no longer benefit from its neutral position. Brittany's main exports included salt from Guérande, wine from the Nantes region, and cereals from Trégor (*Bro-Dreger*) and Penthièvre. The duchy also exported linen and canvas cloth and the extra fine linen used for lace-making in Léon (*Leon*) and Cornouaille became well-known internationally. Breton commerce in general though was woefully underdeveloped, partly because of lack of capital and outdated financial practices. No important Flemish or Italian bank deemed it worth setting up a branch here.

The majority of Breton towns were still hardly more than large villages. Only Nantes and Rennes, with a population of 14,000 and 13,000 respectively, had more than 5,000 inhabitants, and only 7 per cent of Bretons lived in an urban environment. The population in general suffered a decline, possibly by as much as 20 per cent during the end of the fourteenth century and it continued to decrease throughout most of the fifteenth. Only during the last twenty years of that century does the demographic situation seem to improve again. The probable causes were the epidemics of plague and other diseases coupled with the failed harvests mentioned above. The violence and uncertainty of war was another contributory factor.

In light of all this should the Breton dukes be considered particularly poor? In fact Jean IV's income, for example, compared favourably with the dukes of Anjou, Berry and Bourbon. However his revenue was less than that of the duke of Burgundy or of Orléans, and it was positively paltry compared to the vast resources at the French king's disposal. Brittany's position as an independent state was a precarious one and all the duchy could do was play off powerful neighbours against each other through a web of marriage alliances and diplomatic and commercial treaties. The duchy could only hope in the meantime that France persisted in being cursed by weak sovereigns (there had been a series of rulers who were either very young or insane) or else that the war continued to keep the kingdom preoccupied elsewhere.

The situation eventually changed in the mid-fourteenth century when the Hundred Years War finally ended in 1453 and a strong monarch ascended the throne of France in 1461. Unfortunately for Brittany, this coincided with the presence of a weak and ineffectual duke, François II, who also, disastrously, failed to produce a male heir.

The new French king, Louis XI (1461–83), was determined and ruthless and his main objective was to consolidate his power by fully incorporating all his vassal regions into his realm. With the wars ended he now had the military and financial means to do so. His initial attacks on Brittany were on legal issues. The royal lawyers claimed that the duke's conduct in striking gold coins, having relations with foreign states including the pope, and wearing a crown, was illegal and they accused him of encroaching on royal prerogatives.

Brittany was divided on how to deal with the escalating threat from France. The duke was completely dependent on his counsellors and they had split into two camps. The two leaders of these factions were the most important officials in the council, the chancellor and the treasurer, and they were both ambitious and unscrupulous men. Guillaume Chauvin was the chancellor and he was all for having diplomatic relations with France and attempting to appease the French king through legal and diplomatic channels. Initially it was Chauvin's policies which held sway, but as his rival Pierre Landais, the treasurer, expanded his influence and power Chauvin found himself arrested and imprisoned in 1481. The ruthless Landais ensured that he was left there to die of starvation.

Landais' approach to the crisis was to follow a thoroughly anti-French policy and ally with other malcontents in the realm, such as Flanders, England and Burgundy. Brittany thus joined a coalition of chief vassals who united together against a royal bully. The coalition included the duke of Alençon, the count of Armagnac and Charles de Valois who was the king's brother.

Duke François II, on the advice of Landais, welcomed the rebellious Charles in 1466 and Breton troops joined him in 1468 in his attempt to reconquer Normandy which his brother the king had confiscated from him. This military action was disastrous for François and the French army ravaged the Breton marches until the treaty of Ancenis (*Ankiniz*) was signed in September 1468.

Landais' supporters included certain Breton noblemen who had enjoyed positions at the court of the previous French king, Charles VII. They had been dismissed when Louis had purged the court in his endeavour to be completely different from his father. These noblemen fled back to Brittany and sheltered in the ducal court. They pushed for an anti-French policy and external alliances. They added to the dissention at the ducal court because many were jealous of their positions, and there were still numerous important noblemen who had lands in France and preferred Chauvin's approach. This discord within the Breton aristocracy only served to weaken the duchy's position.

By 1480 it was obvious that François was not going to beget sons and this seemed a propitious moment for Louis to obtain Brittany through semi-legal means. He approached Nicole de Penthièvre and bought the rights to the duchy, as stipulated in the first treaty of Guérande 1365, for 50,000 *livres*. This treaty had not foreseen the possibility that both the Montfort and Penthièvre lines might fail to produce male heirs at the same time, but this was what had happened and, so argued Louis, other possibilities could now be considered. Before the opportunity arose however Louis died in 1483, leaving the rule of the kingdom in the hands of his daughter Anne de Beaujeu, as his son Charles VIII was only thirteen. Anne proved to be as capable and determined as her father and she continued his policy of giving succour to the Breton nobles who despised Pierre Landais. His downfall came in 1485 when he was arrested and executed.

François II had now lost his two main councillors but he was still surrounded by powerful men who put their ambitions before the welfare of the duchy, men like Odet d'Agdie the sire of Lescun, who was from Gascony, and Jean de Chalon, prince of Orange. They were hated by many Breton barons and great seigneurial lords, all the more so as they were foreigners. Anne de Beaujeu's policy now paid off as about sixty of these barons now approached her representatives secretly and signed an act acknowledging Charles VIII as the rightful successor to François II. They also asked for military intervention to get rid of the 'foreigners' who surrounded the duke, giving the French regent the perfect excuse to invade Brittany. Thus in spring 1487 the French army successfully captured many towns as far as Vannes. Their failure in the siege of Nantes however was a major setback

and they retreated back to France. But they were back the
following year, fortified by Italian and Swiss mercenaries and the
town of Fougères quickly fell into their hands. The climax of the
war occurred when the king's 15,000 men met the duke's 11,000
at Saint-Aubin-du-Cormier. In the four-hour battle that ensued,
the Breton army was completely annihilated. François had to sue
for peace at the castle of Verger, close to Angers, on 20 August
1488. The main terms were that the duke's daughters could not
marry without the king's consent, various towns and fortresses
were given as pledges, and Charles VIII's claim to the ducal
throne would be re-examined. Soon after signing this peace treaty
François II died in 1488.

The duchy was now in the hands of twelve-year-old Anne, and
the question of her marriage became paramount. Charles VIII
was adamant that he should be Anne's guardian, but Anne had
dismissed her pro-French guardians and taken refuge in Rennes.
French troops still occupied Saint-Malo, Dinan, Fougères and
Saint-Aubin, and in December 1488 the two sides clashed again.
After an initial success the French were gradually pushed back as
Breton forces were reinforced by mercenaries but they still
occupied Brest in Lower Brittany and Dinan, Fougères and
Saint-Malo in Upper Brittany when the treaty of Frankfurt
brought a temporary truce on 22 July 1489. The Bretons took
advantage of this respite to marry Anne to Maximilian of Austria,
although the ceremony was by proxy, on 19 December 1490.
This alliance only succeeded in unleashing the French king's fury
on Brittany as royal forces fiercely attacked once more. Anne
waited in vain for aid from her Austrian ally who had problems
of his own in Flanders and Hungary. It was becoming clear that
Brittany could not withstand France without outside help and
when that was not forthcoming resistance was futile.

The solution in the end was simple: Charles VIII would marry
Anne of Brittany himself. In this way peace would be brought
and the duchy could save face at the same time. The minor matter
of both being already married to somebody else was quickly
resolved by Pope Alexander VI who provided both with
annulments and the marriage took place in December 1491. Thus

the two states were united peacefully. Although this was the end of Brittany's independence to all intents and purposes most of the population at the time welcomed the news of the marriage. After all, Brittany's leaders were divided, her army mediocre and ill-equipped and raising men to fight for her had proven difficult. Nearly half the men in the duke's army were foreigners and several towns had refused to contribute forces. There was a general lack of enthusiasm for the war and all the ordinary people wished for was peace.

Charles VIII proceeded to dismantle the state institutions in Brittany. While keeping some of the duchess's councillors he replaced most with his own, especially in the financial sector, he dismissed the chancery, while the *parlement* was reduced to the level of a judicial court whose final decisions lay in Paris.

The contract between Brittany and France obliged Anne to marry the next heir to the throne when Charles died. This she did in January 1499 marrying Louis XII eight months after Charles' death in April 1498. She was no longer a child and she used those eight months to regain some sovereignty over Brittany. Her first act after Charles's death, the very next day in fact, was to re-establish the duchy's chancery. She liberated the towns and fortresses that were still occupied by royal troops and in the marriage contract with Louis she insisted that Brittany would be inherited by the younger child of the union, and not the eldest who would be king of France. Thus the duchy's own institutions and privileges were reaffirmed and the marriage contract assured that Brittany would have its own dynasty in the future. Anne continued to govern Brittany, via her counsellors, until her death in 1514 but, despite her efforts to ensure the duchy's future independence, she was thwarted by her inability to produce a male heir. Of the eight children only two daughters survived into adulthood.

The eldest, Claude, was made of weaker stuff than her mother and when her husband François of Angoulême became king of France the year after their marriage he obtained concessions from her that meant that Brittany would always be in the hands of the king of France. When duchess Claude died in 1524, her son, who was also the heir to the French throne, became duke of Brittany. Her widower, François I of France, immediately took steps to integrate Brittany fully into the kingdom of France. He obtained an oath of loyalty from the estates of Brittany, although not without lengthy discussions first, and they agreed to accept the dauphin as duke.

Thus the union of France and Brittany was sealed as soon as the dauphin became duke François III of Brittany in 1524. When he was fourteen years old François was taken by his father on a grand tour around France so that he would get to know his kingdom. When he arrived in Brittany he was crowned duke in Rennes and it was decided to formalize the union of the kingdom and the duchy by proclaiming an Act of Union. The year was 1532.

The estates of Brittany were keen to have an official Act of Union so that Brittany's rights would be respected and protected legally. The Act allowed the Breton judicial system to continue and certain privileges enshrined in ancient charters and customs were reaffirmed. The terms of the Act let Brittany keep her estates, her *parlement* and her administrative autonomy. However, when duke François III died in 1536 his younger brother Henri, now heir to the throne, did not adopt the title of duke of Brittany. From henceforth Brittany was simply a province of the kingdom of France.

5

Golden age and civil war (1532–1676)

Brittany's new status as a province did not change matters overnight, the estates had made sure of that, and apart from the loss of the ducal court at Nantes, daily life remained much the same. Indeed Brittany experienced an age of prosperity during the next hundred years or so, despite its annexation to France, and this period has been referred to as Brittany's 'Golden Age'. Evidence of this wealth can still be seen today in the country's churches and chapels that have numerous embellishments and features dating from this time. Even quite modest rural communities constructed lavish charnel houses or added on a magnificent entrance porch to their local church, while others commissioned elaborately carved calvary crosses or built a steeple. Competing with the neighbouring village's church became something of a rural passion, especially in the west.

This affluence was largely due to the development of Brittany's economy as marine trade expanded and the cloth industry in particular flourished. The port of Nantes, served by the Loire river network that gave it access to nearly two-thirds of France, exported thousands of tonnes of wine and it became the second most important port for wine in France. Saint-Malo's principal trade was in cod and Saint-Malo fishermen would set out for Newfoundland to fish and sell the cod to Spain and Italy. Imports included exotic products from the Middle East and boats sailed from the port to the Pacific and the West Indies. By the end of the seventeenth century Saint-Malo was the main French port in terms of traffic volume as it regularly served 3,000 boats.

The increase in the number of boats benefited the sailcloth makers of Locronan (*Lokorn*) and coarse cloth made from hemp was in demand in the West Indies where it was used to clothe slaves. Vitré became the European capital of canvas cloth. The slave-owners and colonials hankered after fresh white linen and this was produced on the northern coast of Brittany, including most of Léon, where a cloth called *crées* was manufactured from flax. Another fine linen cloth called *bretagne* was processed in a vast area from Saint-Brieuc to Pontivy (*Pondivi*).

The textile industry at this time involved peasant farmers weaving the cloth in their own homes. This was a profitable source of extra income in a country where agriculture was still the dominant feature of the economy. One new development in agriculture was the introduction of buckwheat from Asia Minor at the beginning of the sixteenth century; this was a valuable addition to the peasant's staple diet. It produced high yields, even on poor soil, although the harvest was not always dependable. The peasants kept the buckwheat for their own consumption, which then released the other grain grown, mostly wheat and rye, for the market. Buckwheat escaped taxation for a long time and the peasants avoided the tolls associated with the seigneurial mill and oven by using handmills and baking the buckwheat into the flat pancake *galettes* that are now considered so typical of Breton cuisine.

Brittany's period of economic expansion is in marked contrast to the stagnation that France suffered in the seventeenth century. This was partly due to its geographical position as the peninsula was able relatively easily to switch its commercial efforts to the new economic powers of Europe, England and Holland, when the markets of Spain and Portugal slumped. Economic success was reflected in the growth of Brittany's population, which increased from about 1,500,000 at the end of the fifteenth century, to reach 2,000,000 by 1680–90. The greatest increase was in the towns and ports, with Nantes growing to 40,000 by the late seventeenth century and Saint-Malo reaching 25,000.

The desire to decorate and extend the local church and erect calvary crosses, referred to above, was not only a result of the increasing prosperity, it was also a manifestation of the religious feeling that was sweeping the land as the church's Counter-Reformation measures began to take effect. One priest who did much to revitalize the church at a local level was Michel Le Nobletz (1577–1652). He preached in Breton in the west and inspired the illiterate peasants with his brightly painted pictures, the *taolennoù*. Father Julien Maunoir (1606–83) also contributed by organizing hundreds of missions and writing a catechism manual. Like Le Nobletz he realized the importance of using the people's own language and he compiled a Breton–French dictionary, the first text in modern Breton.

This golden age of Brittany however was marred by a civil war and a rebellion, both of which had an adverse effect on the growth in prosperity and population although the province did recover afterwards.

In 1589, after nearly a hundred years of peace, Brittany was dragged into France's Wars of Religion. Up until then Brittany had avoided the conflict with the Protestant Huguenots which had ravaged much of France. There were very few Protestants in Brittany; a few nobles, such as the prominent Rohan and Laval families, had converted, and there was a small community in the region of Dinan, but their presence had not caused any disturbance. But when a group of powerful noblemen established the Catholic League in 1584 to try and prevent France from having a Protestant king, one of the main leaders was the duke of Mercoeur, who was also the governor of Brittany. When king Henry III died in 1589, naming the Huguenot Henry of Navarre as his rightful heir, the Catholic League swung into action with Mercoeur as one of the main leaders.

Ostensibly the war that the leaguers launched was on grounds of religion, but in Brittany it quickly degenerated into a civil war as different factions fought each other under the guise of leaguer and royalist labels. The conflict was the opportunity for rival gentry families to settle old scores, for peasants to attack the gentry, for the rural poor to attack the towns and for the urban bourgeoisie to strive for a return to greater municipal independence (Saint-Malo created a quasi-independent republic under League protection in 1589). The whole scenario was further complicated by the arrival of Spanish and English troops who came to assist the leaguer and royalist forces respectively. In addition to this there were several brigands roaming the countryside adding to the general lawlessness and the country suffered a series of bad harvests.

Merceour's base was the staunchly leaguer city of Nantes where a judicial court was set up to rival the *parlement* at Rennes which was, along with the town itself, strictly for the king. Many of Brittany's noblemen, who were suspicious of Mercoeur's ambitions and increasing power, also supported the royalist cause. Merceour's first action was to try to secure the main towns of Upper Brittany, but no sooner had he captured Rennes than he lost it again as soon as he had left. He was more successful with Fougères but failed to seize Vitré, even though he had the support of the surrounding region.

In 1590, with the death of Cardinal Bourbon, the Catholic League lost its contender to the throne. One possible alternative was Isabella, granddaughter of Henry II, who was the daughter of Philip II, the king of Spain, so it was no surprise that Mercoeur appealed to Philip for help. In October of that year, 7,000 Spanish troops disembarked at Saint-Nazaire (*Sant-Nazer*) and immediately headed for the royalist town of Blavet. By the end of December Hennebont had also fallen to the leaguer forces. The *parlement* at Rennes panicked and begged the king to appeal to England for reinforcements. English troops arrived in May the following year and their presence helped the prince of Dombes (now the governor of Brittany, Mercoeur having been dismissed), capture leaguer Guingamp (*Gwengamp*) on 3 June 1591. The following May, Mercoeur with the Spanish defeated the French king's army at the battle of Craon in Maine. This was the height of Merceour's success. He assembled the estates of Brittany but hesitated in attacking Rennes. He grudgingly allowed the Spanish to build a fort on the Crozon (*Kraozon*) peninsula at Roscanvel (*Roskañvel*), opposite the royalist port of Brest. Mutual distrust and disagreements between the ex-governor and his Spanish allies meant that Craon's success was never properly exploited.

The following year, 1593, king Henry IV converted to Catholicism. The main reason for the Catholic League's grievances no longer existed and many leaguer noblemen in France flocked over to the king's side. There were some die-hard leaguers, however, who claimed that the king's conversion was a sham, and Merceour, probably for his own political ambitions rather than religious convictions, insisted on holding out. Brittany had to suffer five more years of fighting.

In 1594 the king sent the current governor of Brittany, Marshal d'Aumont, to launch an expedition on Lower Brittany. He captured Morlaix and Quimper and seized the Spanish fort at Roscanvel in November. The following year d'Aumont captured Corlay (*Korle*) but he was killed at the siege of Comper castle. The war dragged on as it continued to play out a multitude of local skirmishes where both sides suffered losses. More Spanish forces arrived in 1597 and in December of that year the estates of Brittany appealed to Henry IV to provide more assistance. The king decided that enough was enough and came himself, at the head of his army, to Brittany in 1598. He captured the leaguer stronghold of Dinan and finally Mercoeur gave himself up at Angers in April. Securing his authority in the province Henry IV found himself in Nantes in April and May when he signed the famous Edict of Nantes, which allowed the Protestants freedom of worship. He also signed the treaty of Vervins which expelled the Spanish from Breton soil. The League war in Brittany had finally come to an end.

Mercoeur was banished from Brittany and he spent the rest of his life fighting the Turks in Hungary. The city of Nantes suffered a further loss in its status as the chamber of accounts, the *bureau des trésoriers généraux* (public revenue office) and the university were all decamped to Rennes. The leaguer *parlemantaires* of Nantes were quickly integrated into the *parlement* at Rennes. Protestantism in Brittany, on the other hand, despite the concessions of the Edict of Nantes, lost ground quickly.

The noble families who had embraced the new faith failed to pass it on to the next generation and by 1620 there remained only nine Protestant *temples* in Brittany.

One result of the League war was to strengthen the bond between Brittany and France. The war had not been a Breton resistance to French authority in any way and now the people looked to the king more than ever to restore peace and prosperity to the land. Henry IV showed clemency and his main targets for punishment were the brigands who were still causing havoc. He destroyed certain fortresses like the castles of Corlay and Broons (*Bronn*), along with the fortifications of Rennes that had made that city almost impenetrable.

The *parlement* of Rennes, which had shown such loyalty to the king during the League war, had been created by Henry II in 1554. There had been a high judicial court of sorts in Brittany since 1491 with the supreme court of appeal being in Paris, but by the mid-sixteenth century, as France annexed more territories, it was no longer practical for the *parlement* of Paris to deal with all regional appeals and so eventually all the main provinces had a *parlement* each. The king took precautions to ensure that the Breton *parlement* would not be too partial to the province. Of the thirty-two councillors, sixteen had to be non-Breton and he stipulated that the president should also be non-Breton. His efforts were in vain however, as many of the non-Bretons who bought offices in the *parlement* came from the neighbouring provinces of Anjou and Maine, usually acquired land in the region, quickly put down roots and were ready to plead for Breton interests.

Ostensibly the *parlement* was a court of justice, dealing with appeals from lesser tribunals and seigneurial courts, but it also had an administrative role which increased as time went by. It scrutinized all regulations emenating from the king and any royal decision was not accepted as law until it had been registered by the *parlement*. This institution, comprising mostly noblemen and a few rich bourgeois, fiercely defended any act it saw as an encroachment on its privileges, such as the introduction of or increase in certain taxes. The *parlement* at Rennes was eventually housed in the *Palais* that was built in 1618–55 in a typically French neo-classical style.

Another institution that endeavoured to protect Breton interests against royal control was the estates. Originally this institution had been assembled when the duke wanted to impose taxes on land outside the immediate ducal demesne, and the imposition of taxes by the king was one of the main issues that the estates continued to discuss as a provincial body. Using 'the ancient custom of Brittany' as the legal base for their arguments, they did their best to defend the interests of Brittany against too much interference from central government. Each year the king would attempt to negotiate the annual sum of taxes to be collected and he did not always get the desired sum; for example in 1580 Henry III asked the estates of Brittany to provide him with 300,000 *livres*, but he only received 100,000 that year. The estates also protected the other fundamental liberties of Brittany, which included the right for Bretons to be tried only at Breton courts of law, that only Bretons would be appointed to ecclesiastical posts, and that no armed service outside Brittany could be requested of Bretons. Furthermore no changes could be made to the institutions of the province without first securing the estates' agreement.

The president of the estates was the governor, and he was meant to represent the king in Brittany. The governor's duties were to implement the royal laws and keep the peace in the province. In the sixteenth century the post was held by men who had close family ties and property in Brittany, such as members of the Laval family from Châteaubriant. The duke of Mercoeur was married to the heiress of Penthièvre and his son-in-law, the duke of Vendôme, also became governor of Brittany. In 1631 however the situation changed completely when one of the most important men in the kingdom of France was appointed governor of Brittany.

As Louis XIII's chief minister, cardinal Richelieu was largely responsible for transforming France into a highly centralized state. He sought to restrain the power of the nobility on the king's behalf and he was concerned about the provincial governorships where the governor, although in theory representing the king, could in reality be in control of the province himself almost like a separate fiefdom. The duke of Mercoeur's actions during the League war was proof of that, and Richelieu did his best to curtail the governors' powers. In 1614 there were sixteen provincial governorships but Richelieu made sure that by his death in 1642 there were only four. When the duke of Vendôme became involved in a conspiracy against the cardinal, it was the perfect excuse for Richelieu to take the governorship of Brittany himself and there is some evidence that he was invited to do so by the Breton estates.

Richelieu was governor of Brittany from 1631 until his death in 1642 but he left the day-to-day running of the province to his cousin the lieutenant general the marquis of La Meilleraye and he never visited the country himself. Nevertheless, Richelieu was interested in Brittany for strategic reasons. In 1618 the fortress of Blavet had been reinforced and rebaptized Port-Louis (*Porzh-Loeiz*) as it could be used as a base against the rebellious Huguenot stronghold of La Rochelle further down the west coast of France. Richelieu now saw the potential of Brittany's coastal defences and naval forces in general and he put in motion a programme of reinforcement. Since 1626 he had been the Admiral of France and he had also made himself the *'surintendant général de la navigation et commerce de France'* and in this guise he intended to control maritime commerce. His attempt to abolish the special naval privileges that most of France's coastal provinces enjoyed met opposition in Brittany like elsewhere. The *parlement* made it clear that his passports were not viable there and the estates argued that maritime control of the country was a ducal right that had been been inherited by the provincial governors. This opposition resolved itself when Richelieu created a separate admiralty for Brittany under the supervision of the governor, being, from 1631, himself. As the admiral, Richelieu ordered that every port had to build one ship for royal services. A new dockyard and arsenal were established in Brest and in 1636 the port produced seventeen ships and frigates. Brest developed still further under Richelieu's successor, Colbert, who made it the maritime capital of the kingdom.There he established a school of gunnery, a college of marine guards, a school of hydrography and a school for marine engineers.

In 1640 Richelieu attempted to increase his control by creating seven royal maritime courts in Brittany. The *parlement* at Rennes expressed misgivings at this before finally registering the decision but the estates were vehemently opposed to this development. The crown succumbed to their pressure in 1643 and the courts were abolished. However, they were reinstated in 1691.

This attempt to bypass local judicial proceedings was just another example of the effort of the king to concentrate power in his own hands and diminish the power of the feudal nobility. Richelieu started the process of circumventing local officials by using centrally appointed men, *intendants*, who were directly accountable to the crown. They were sent on special missions to the provinces so, for example, in 1638 the *intendant* Lasnier authorized the arrest of a gentryman who was guilty of banditry around Saint-Cast (*Sant-Kast*) and proceeded to pronounce the death sentence on him without consulting the Breton *parlement*, who protested against this infringement. The *intendants* were also used increasingly in the financial sphere as a way of collecting taxes more efficiently. This new development did not happen without protest. The attempt in 1636 by an *intendant* at the estates at Nantes to convert the *arrière-ban* (the gentry's duty to provide military service) to money, and thus indirectly tax a class who were usually exempt, provoked a three-day riot.

The *intendants* were extremely unpopular and, as the crown continued to increase its centralist tendencies, the discontent of the noblemen and traditional office holders throughout France, whose powers and privileges were being eroded daily, finally erupted in 1648 into a rebellion called the Fronde.

The *parlement* at Rennes had already remonstrated with the king (the ten-year-old Louis XIV) about the appointment of the *intendant* Louis de Coëtlogon de Méjusseaume in 1647 and in 1648, and now this protest became swallowed up in the general grievances of the Fronde. The estates in Brittany, on the other hand, supported the royal government.

The Fronde insurgency was quashed in 1653 and the main repercussion for Brittany was that the incident served to convince the young king that direct rule was best. It was during Louis XIV's reign that absolutism was consolidated as the independent power of the great nobles was broken and the centralist government was reinforced. For Brittany this meant the effective imposition of higher taxes and an increasing number of *intendants* who proceeded to control various spheres of Breton life as they sought to integrate Brittany even further into French administration. The estates found themselves under growing pressure to produce higher and higher annual sums, called the *don gratuit*, to the crown, until in 1671 the governor of Brittany, the duke of Chaulnes, was able to persuade the estates to vote the complete sum for that year without any debate or discussion.

The high military expenditure on various wars and the growing administrative costs of bureaucratic development, along with the royal court's increasing consumption, had turned the French monarchical state into a machine for levying taxes. The main burden of the taxes, as always, fell on the poor, the rural mass of the population and the urban lower classes, and in fact the process of deciding on the amount to be collected was very often a balancing act to see how much could be extracted before they revolted. And revolt they did: France was beset by uprisings for fifty years from the early 1620s to the mid 1670s. Brittany's turn came in 1675.

The 1675 rebellion was provoked by the chief minister Colbert's decree that all legal actions had to be recorded on stamped paper. He also reimposed taxes on tobacco and pewter vessels. This act affected the towns directly as centres of commerce and justice. The uprising began in Bordeaux, but as soon as news of the insurrection reached Brittany in April the city of Rennes reacted by ransacking the tobacco and stamped paper offices. The mayor and the local militia dispersed the rioters who were made up of porters, craftsmen, journeymen and labourers, but the insurrection spread to Dinan, Dol, Guingamp, Lamballe (*Lambal*), Nantes and Vannes. Disturbances flared up again in Rennes later in the month when there were rumours that the *gabelle*, the hated salt tax, would be imposed on Brittany. News of the rioting soon spread to Lower Brittany where there were plenty of reasons to rebel. The financial pressure placed on the people by the seigneurs had continued to increase since the middle of the century because the noblemen themselves were feeling the pinch. Aristocratic, bourgeois and ecclesiastical landlords had all been increasing their own tithes. The peasants of Cornouaille were hit hardest as they lacked the textile industry that was helping to boost the income of many peasants in Léon and elsewhere. Thus when the marquis of La Coste, the king's lieutenant in Lower Brittany, arrived at Châteaulin (*Kastellin*) in June to levy new taxes, the news of the riots in Rennes and the rumours about the *gabelle* had preceded him. The people erupted spontaneously, the marquis was badly wounded and gangs of angry peasants attacked manor houses and castles in the regions of Quimper, Pont-l'Abbé (*Pont-'n-Abad*) and in the hinterland of Cornouaille. Charters were burnt and gentry folk were killed.

Among the leaders were minor officers of justice, better-off peasants, inn keepers and even some minor gentry. One of the most remarkable leaders was Sébastien Le Balp, a notary from Carhaix who had been imprisoned for being in debt. He organized a regular troop of men called the *Bonnedou ru* (red bonnets) and the whole uprising came to be known by this name. With 10,000 men he captured the castle of Kergoet. The previously spontaneous revolt became more efficient as the leaders now took control of communications and led attacks against castles. The towns themselves began to feel threatened; at Guingamp, Morlaix and Brest they mounted a guard on the ramparts. Tax collectors were attacked, their goods destroyed and their papers burnt; noblemen were massacred at Briec (*Brieg*), Chateaulin, Combrit (*Kombrid*), Douarnenez, Pont-l'Abbé, Ploemeur (*Plañvour*), Plonéour and Gourin. In July and August the movement moved from west Cornouaille to east Cornouaille, the Vannetais and the Poher (*Poc'hêr*) area, where general assemblies were formed. These assemblies drew up lists of grievances and made plans for social and economic reforms. Several codes were drawn up, eight of which survive, voicing their hopes for reforms such as the abolition of various taxes and certain feudal rights, for example the landlords' power to force peasants to use the seigneurial mill exclusively.

In September Le Balp was assassinated at Poullaouen by the marquis of Montgaillard. The duke of Chaulnes arrived with soldiers and the rebellion was suppressed for good. The instigators were tortured, sent to the galleys, exiled or executed. Certain parishes had fines imposed on them and their church bell towers destroyed. The participants were broken at the wheel, others were hanged. In Rennes thirty people were killed on the wheel or hanged and the quarter of la rue Haute was razed to the ground and its inhabitants left homeless. Although the troops sent to quell the rebellion did not have to fight battles as such they were used as a means of punishment as 5,000 of them were stationed at Rennes for the winter where the town was expected to provide them with everything. Other troops were quartered elsewhere in Brittany for the winter and they pillaged and looted as they wished, acting like an occupying army in enemy territory. It is estimated that the damage caused to the country by these soldiers far outweighed the destruction of the rebellion. The *parlement* was exiled to Vannes for fifteen years, which only added to Rennes' misery. Finally, in February 1676, the king relented and withdrew his troops from Brittany as he needed them to fight in his campaign against Holland. The brutal repression left its mark on Brittany and many impoverished peasants joined the bands of brigands that roamed the countryside for years to come. The efficient suppression of the *Bonnedou ru* rebellion only served to confirm the iron grip that the French crown now had on all its provinces.

6

Economic decline and the onset of the Revolution (1670–1789)

While Brittany ended the seventeenth century firmly under royal control, the subsequent years of the eighteenth century saw the province play its part in undermining the authority of the king during the events that preceded the French Revolution. This century also witnessed a decline in Brittany's economic expansion and a deceleration in the population growth.

Although the overall economy of Brittany can be said to have suffered a downturn during this period there were notable exceptions, in particular the success of Nantes and Brest and the new port of Lorient (*An Oriant*). During the second half of the eighteenth century the merchants of Nantes developed a thriving trade with the Caribbean. They had moved on from the traditional products of wine, salt, wheat and fish and now dealt in indigo, tobacco, cotton, coffee, cocoa and cane sugar. However, the mainstay of Nantes' trade, which made countless merchants extremely prosperous, was slaves. It has been calculated that up to 350,000 slaves were transported to the colonies in ships from Nantes during the eighteenth century, making it the principal slave port of France. The city also became one of the great centres for printed calico, employing 5,000 workers, and the population of Nantes doubled to nearly 90,000. Although the city's wealth did extend to its hinterland the main access to this was along the river Loire and the communities that benefited most from trading and exchanging goods with Nantes were in Anjou and Poitiou rather than in Brittany.

The fortunes of Brest were closely linked with the French navy and the royal arsenal and ship-building yards here employed thousands. Indeed, the ship-yards of Brest, along with those of Nantes and Saint-Malo, made Brittany the main region in France for naval construction during the eighteenth century. Chosen by the French chief minister Colbert in the previous century to be the royal naval centre, Brest was an artificial French enclave in the heart of Breton speaking Brittany. Its population was swelled by immigrants, and while many of these had come from other parts of Brittany, 25 per cent of the inhabitants in 1750 were foreigners. By the end of the century Brest's population was 30,000.

Another of Colbert's creations was the port of Lorient. In 1664 Colbert had founded the East Indies Company in an attempt to develop trade with the colonies. Two years later the company bought some wasteland at the mouth of the river Blavet (*Ar Blavezh*) in order to establish a settlement for their headquarters. By 1750 Lorient's population was nearly 20,000, 28 per cent of whom were foreigners, mostly Dutch and Italian. The port traded in colonial goods such as coffee, pepper, cinnamon, printed calico, muslin, silk, tea and porcelain.

The French authorities could thus provide an impetus for economic development, as happened at Brest and Lorient, but French economic practices could also have a devastating effect on Brittany's economy. Until the latter part of the seventeenth century Brittany had been left alone to follow its own economic path but with the advent of Colbert and his successors Breton industries and markets increasingly felt the effects of their policies. One of the most detrimental was the decision to impose heavy taxes on foreign woollen cloth. The aim of this tax was to stimulate the French domestic woollen cloth industry but the effects on Brittany's exports were disastrous.

The traditional exchange of goods had been Breton linen (in particular the cloth *crées* produced in the Léon region) for British woollen cloth; so as the taxes steadily rose many British ships no longer came to ports like Saint-Malo and Morlaix to sell their wares and thus no longer bought Breton linen to take home with them. The Breton estates complained to the king about the situation, claiming that Brittany should be exempt from the import duties under the conditions of the Act of Union of 1532. The royal council's retort was that the development of the woollen industry was to the benefit of all the provinces and that

Brittany's claim was invalid. The situation was made even worse in 1687 when woollen cloth was henceforth only allowed into France through two specific ports, neither of which were in Brittany. As relations between Britain and France deteriorated Breton exports suffered further when Britain, in retaliation, increased its import duties on French products culminating in a complete ban on all French imports from 1678–85. Brittany was not able to regain the British market in the eighteenth century, despite the subsequent reduction in taxes, as Britain in the meantime had fulfilled its needs by buying Dutch and German linen and developing its own linen industry in Ireland.

Nevertheless the textile industry also produced cloths that were not so dependent on the British market. The fine quality *bretagne* still had its colonial markets, especially in Latin America, and the production of this cloth steadily increased until 1775 when the sea routes were closed due to the American War of Independence. Breton canvas cloth still found its way on to the backs of slaves in the Caribbean and the sail-cloth makers in the parishes south of Rennes doubled their production in the second half of the eighteenth century in their effort to supply the ship builders.

When Saint-Malo lost its linen market in Britain and its trade was affected by war it attempted to adapt to the situation in two ways. Some enterprising individuals developed privateering as a solution and the port became infamous for its *corsaires*. About fifty privateering ships a year operated from Saint-Malo between 1688 and 1713. The other initiative was the founding of a company in 1698 to develop trade with the Pacific coast of South America while another group of Saint-Malo tradesmen founded their own company in 1712 to trade with the East Indies. However, after about twenty years of success during which Saint-Malo was the main French port for the import of silver, the Spaniards closed their outlet to South America. The East Indian company also became unprofitable after it lost its monopoly in 1719. The traders of Saint-Malo, unlike those of Nantes, had failed to realize that the future lay in the Caribbean. The town's population of 25,000 in 1700 had receded to 15,000 by 1750.

Despite some notable successes in Brittany's economy the overall picture is still one of a decline in general prosperity and this is largely due to the fact that the country's economy was still overwhelmingly agricultural. There were no new significant developments in agricultural techniques in the eighteenth century, and although the rate of population increase had slowed down the actual number of people was still rising and it was becoming increasingly difficult for the land to provide enough food. This was exacerbated by the deteriorating climate as periods of drought followed by excessive rains were common between 1692 and1789. Another contributing factor was the escalation of new diseases as, for example, sailors and soldiers arriving in Brest brought in typhus and syphilis (virtually unknown in Brittany before 1532) and other foreign infections found their way in via the ports that traded with the colonies. Brittany's population, which had increased by 43 per cent in less than two centuries, now increased by only 10 per cent to reach 2,200,000 in 1801.

The repression after the 1675 rebellion (see previous chapter) and the rebuff of the estates by the crown ten years later regarding the duties on woollen cloth imports (see above) demonstrated to Brittany the extent to which it was now integrated into the French kingdom, both economically and politically. It was the last province in France to be provided with a permanent *intendant* in 1689 and this direct representative of royal power was accepted without a murmur. The post of governor now became honorific and the province was governed directly by the *intendant* and the commander in chief, both appointed by the king. Yet as soon as the absolutist monarch Louis XIV died in 1715 the Breton estates gained confidence and began to voice their opinions loudly again. At their meeting in Dinan in 1717 they refused to grant the *don gratuit* without discussing the amount first.

Their action was not without justification: the financial pressure of increasing taxes levied to pay for Louis XIV's constant warfare had become intolerable. The enormous amounts demanded by Versailles had obliged Brittany to spend revenues four years in advance and by 1709 the province as a whole was 2,700,000 *livres* in debt. This is not to say however that Louis XIV was demanding more of Brittany than any other part of his kingdom. In fact Brittany was exempt from the much hated salt tax, the *gabelle*, and the *taille*. However this exemption was more than made up for, as far as the ordinary peasant was concerned, by the higher rates of other taxes such as the *fouage* (land tax) and *devoir* (a tax on drink). These taxes were levied and collected by the estates themselves and thus the estates' protests to the crown about unfair taxation was as much about protecting their own privileges and exemptions as it was for the benefit of the ordinary Breton.

The response of the commander in chief of Brittany, the Marshal de Montesquiou, to the Dinan estates' demands, was to dissolve the assembly after three days. But eight months later the regent intervened and the estates were recalled to Dinan in 1718. The *parlement* in Rennes supported the estates and forbade all Bretons from paying any taxes that had not been agreed upon by the estates at Dinan until they had received an answer from the crown. Montesquiou's response this time was to expel the *parlement*. This only served to harden the attitudes of the Bretons who drew up a programme of what they believed were Brittany's liberties and rights under the Act of Union. The programme was signed by 500 mainly minor noblemen, including one marquis de Pontcallec. The leaders of the group turned to Spain for support and the action escalated into a plot to steal the regency from Philippe d'Orléans (who was in charge as Louis XV was still an infant), and give the kingdom to the king of Spain, Philip V, who was a grandson of Louis XIV. It did not take long for the regency police to discover the conspiracy and although the Parisian participants had withdrawn in time or escaped to Spain, the four main Breton leaders were arrested. Feelings were running high in Brittany: in July 1719 there were poor riots at Lamballe, and a tax collector was attacked by the crowd in Vitré. In an effort to prevent these troubles from escalating Orléans deemed it prudent to have the four Breton conspirators executed in Nantes on 16 March 1720. The result was that the four were transformed into martyrs by the people from west Vannetais to Cornouaille. The marquis of Pontcallec was immortalized in several songs and when he appeared in the ballad bearing his name in the *Barzaz Breiz* the following century his name was to be entrenched in the folk memory of Breton patriots. He is glorified as a dashing young nobleman fighting for Breton rights; in truth it seems that he was a bitter minor gentry man in his forties who ruthlessly exploited his tenants who despised him.

The following thirty years saw relative political calm as less belligerent commanders in chief were appointed to Brittany. The estates used this calm to gradually increase their powers as they established an intermediary commission to carry out administrative duties in between the sittings of the estates. This commission became responsible for building and repairing main roads and obtained the authority to collect and control funds in order to lodge and maintain troops. The commission enabled the estates to control the collection of taxes as they used this as a condition of agreeing to the king's demands.

This quiet period was disrupted in 1762 when the commander in chief, the duke of Aiguillon, attempted to force through the king's demand for yet another *vingtième* (twentieth) tax on the estates of Brittany. The *vingtième* tax had been established for the first time in 1749 causing much trepidation and discussion in the estates. For once this was a tax which applied to the nobility as well, it was a 5 per cent tax levied on the net income of all landowners, in spite of their usual prerogatives. A second *vingtième* was imposed in 1756 and a third in 1760. This tax was extremely unpopular and many of the provincial *parlements*, including the one at Rennes, protested, along with the *parlement* of Paris. However the estates of Brittany this time were not unanimously against the tax. The first estate, the clergy, who were exempt from the tax anyway, supported the king, and the third estate, who usually bore the brunt of the taxes, were not adverse to seeing the nobility of the second estate having to contribute for a change. Thus, as he had the accord of two out of three of the estates, Aiguillon felt justified in claiming that the *vingtième* had been accepted. Furious, the second estate appealed to the *parlement* for support, and what began as a protest against tax turned into a general grievance about Aiguillon and the way he was governing Brittany. In particular he was criticized for his road-building programme that used peasants as labourers during harvest time, and he was charged with spending unnecessarily on a militia and coastal guards during times of peace. The accusations against Aiguillon in June 1764 were led by the public prosecutor of the *parlement* of Rennes, Caradeuc de La Chalotais. The *parlement* decided in July to break off all relations with the commander in chief, despite reprimands from the king, and they repeated their objections to Aiguillon. The estates met at Nantes in October 1764 where they decided to oppose the collection of the tax of two *sols* a *livre*. They appealed once again to the *parlement* and once again the *parlement* ratified their decision and refused to register the tax or allow its collection. The estates and the *parlement* were working in partnership, unlike in other provinces, and it was proving to be very effective. In March 1765 the Breton *parlement* was summoned to Versailles where they were rebuked by the king. The *parlement*'s response to this was to resign, more or less en masse, in April and May. This disobedience and discontent was not unique to Brittany; the *parlement* of Pau also resigned in April 1765.

In November 1765 the Breton public prosecutor La Chalotais was accused of calumny and he was arrested and imprisoned. This was a mistake on Louis XV's part. The absolute power that his predecessor Louis XIV had achieved had been eroded and it was no longer possible to imprison a nobleman, and a distinguished magistrate at that, on a royal whim. This lack of respect for basic legal principles was considered an outrage and the *parlement* of Paris and all the *parlements* of the provinces came out in support of the Bretons. They all sent remonstrances to the king about the matter, and such was the pressure that the case against La Chalotais was dropped in December 1766, although he was not released. The duke of Aiguillon retired from Brittany.

This was not the end of the affair because when the *parlement* of Brittany was recalled in 1769 one of its first actions was to call for a law suit against Aiguillon. He was meant to be tried by the

Court of Peers at the *parlement* of Paris but at the last moment
the king stepped in and halted the trial. This action of preventing
the course of justice by a king was wholly unacceptable. It was
perceived as an authoritarian act and all the *parlements* protested
with the estates of Brittany leading a violent indictment against
Aiguillon in September 1770. The royal government's response
in 1771 was to restrict the *parlements'* right to remonstrance and
they reacted by promptly going on strike. The magistrates were
exiled and all the *parlements*, including the Paris *parlement*, were
dissolved. New men were put in their place and the reformed
parlements, with less ability to remonstrance, were operational
from the end of 1771. The finance minister took advantage of
these weakened *parlements* to ensure rigorous collection of taxes
and to make the *vingtième* tax permanent. Brittany received a
new commander in chief and *intendant* who had to carry out
these reforms. Inevitably, when the estates met at Morlaix in
1772 they protested and refused to vote through the taxes.

In 1774 Louis XV died and La Chalotais, after nine years'
imprisonment in various castles, was finally released. The
members of *parlement* who had been dismissed were now
reinstated although they were more restricted than before. In
1788 any power the *parlements* had was further reduced by the
keeper of the Seals, Lamoignon, when he withdrew their right to
register and remonstrance altogether and established the *grands
bailliages*. The three *grands bailliages* based in Rennes, Nantes
and Quimper were now deemed to be the last resort in judging
many cases, and thus the Breton *parlement* was by-passed
completely. Further measures were taken by the chief minister
August Brienne to confine the *parlements* to purely judicial
functions and thus break any political power they had. These
edicts were imposed on the *parlement* of Paris by the king and in
the provinces the commanders in chief had to force the same laws
through with a show of arms. Louis XVI ordered that all the
parlements should be dissolved for the time being. This political
coup by the monarch caused an uproar as each *parlement* was
outraged.

In Rennes, in June, the *parlement* palace was surrounded by soldiers to prevent the *parlement* from assembling there, so they met in the Cuillé hotel instead. The troops were met by an angry crowd who supported the *parlement*. The turmoil spread throughout Brittany and the estates decided to send a delegation of twelve to Versailles to complain about the exile of their sister institution. They were welcomed in Paris by those who opposed the crown, but the authorities promptly imprisoned them in the Bastille. This action only fuelled the anger in Brittany and the disturbances spread throughout Brittany, echoing what was occurring in the rest of the kingdom. The crown's reputation was in tatters and in August the chief minister had to admit that the royal coffers were empty. The monarchy was in crisis and the king finally bowed to pressure and agreed to call the Estates General on 1 May 1789.

The Estates General, which had not been summoned since 1614, was a body that represented the three estates throughout the kingdom of France and could be summoned by the king when he deemed it necessary. Usually the crown wished to impose new taxes and thus called them together to get their cooperation, and the Estates General in the past had also used the occasion as an opportunity to counsel and advise the king. However, the absolutist reigns of the previous monarchs had made most taxes permanent and succeeded in raising money without having to consult the Estates General, but Louis XVI was in crisis and had no choice.

There were differences of opinion about what format the Estates General should take. Some assumed it would operate as it had almost a 180 years previously, when the three estates met and voted separately. This meant that the first and second estate could easily veto the third's vote even though the third estate, ostensibly, represented 98 per cent of the king's subjects. The deputies who sat with the third estate mostly came from urban bourgeoisie backgrounds and this new middle class had grown in importance, wealth and political maturity since 1614. They felt that they were not fairly represented, especially as the first and second estate were exempt from most taxes, and they wished to see their numbers increase and for the estates to sit and vote together.

The middle class in Brittany was in full agreement with this stance, even more so as they felt that the argument brandished in the Breton estates' meetings about preserving the ancient rights and privileges of Brittany was in reality more to do with preserving the privileges and tax exemptions of the aristocracy. Like the rest of France the Enlightenment had reached Brittany and there was a growing number of people with access to new ideas and philosophies. During the 1770s scores of literary societies and reading chambers had multiplied in even quite small places like Dinan, Saint-Brieuc, Quimper and Lesneven. There were important literary centres at Morlaix and Saint-Malo. The reading chamber at Nantes, founded in 1759, had a library of 10,000 volumes and 125 members. Rennes, as well as a flourishing reading chamber founded in 1775, also had five publishers, sixteen presses and six bookshops. Members of the reading clubs received books and journals and discussed politics. They talked about the philosophers and the new ideas and some read forbidden books smuggled in from Holland and England. The foreign immigrants in Brest and Lorient and the merchants who came to Nantes all contributed to the flow of new thought coming into the country.

The issue of what form the Estates General should take was hotly debated in the literary chambers and reading clubs and there was anger when the *parlement* at Rennes followed the example of the Paris and other provincial *parlements* and proclaimed, as they registered the royal declaration summoning the Estates General, that they too insisted on the 1614 format. Those who opposed keeping the old order became vociferous and throughout France they were able to put so much pressure on the government that finally a compromise was met in December 1788. The government agreed that the number representing the third estate should be equal to the other two estates – that is, there would be 600 deputies representing the third estate in the Estates General. However, it left unresolved the matter of how they should meet and vote. The noblemen of Brittany were

vehemently opposed to this increase in the number of representatives for the third estate and they responded by orchestrating a
'popular' riot in Rennes. Dayworkers, domestic servants and
porters were egged on to march in a crowd to shouts of 'long live
the nobility'. They came head to head with a crowd of law
students who supported the third estate and the ensuing hours of
conflict left three dead and dozens wounded. As a result, the
commander in chief of Brittany suspended the estates on
14 February 1789.

In order to choose the deputies who would convene in the
Estates General in Versailles a series of elections took place. The
country was divided into units (called *sénéchaussée* or *bailliage*),
of which there were twenty-three in Brittany, and each unit would
send a representative from each estate to the Estates General. The
clergy and nobility voted directly for their representative to the
sénéchaussée, but for the commoners, the third estate, there were
two levels of elections. At the first level, in the rural
communities, the deputies were elected to the parish assembly,
and in the towns it was the guilds and corporations who chose a
delegate for the city assembly. It was then the parish assembly
and city assembly who chose the delegates for the *sénéchaussée*
in a second round of elections. At each stage of the elections
cahiers de doléances (statements of grievances) were drawn up
and they were then combined together to form one *cahier* per
region. Eventually, all the grievances were amalgamated to
produce one *cahier géneral* which would then be presented to the
king.

In February 1789 the electoral assemblies were supposed to
meet in the chief towns of the *sénéchaussées* to choose their
delegates and draw up their *cahier de doléances*. This is what
happened in the most of France but the stubbornness of the
Breton nobility had brought the process to a halt in Brittany. The
noblemen were adamant that the deputies should be chosen by
the estates, and when this demand was rejected they refused to
participate in the election on the grounds that the third estate had
no right to have an independent voice. By mid-March, however,
the nobility were resigned to the elections following the set

procedure. They also consented to the doubling of the number of third estate deputies to forty-four, but only on condition that these reforms would be enacted by the Breton estates themselves. However, the commander in chief promptly reminded them that the Breton estates had been suspended (because of the riot in Rennes). Disgusted by this attitude, the nobility and the high clergy refused to participate in the elections.

Thus it was that when the Estates General assembled in May 1789 all of the representatives from Brittany were exclusively from the third estate. They comprised seventeen lawyers, ten administrators, nine merchants, four rich labourers, three mayors and one doctor. When they arrived in Paris they were greeted by cheering crowds as it had been expected that they would not come at all. With such a high proportion of urban bourgeoisie deputies it was no wonder that the Bretons gained the reputation of being radical in the following eventful days.

7

Revolution and counter-revolution (1789–1815)

As the Breton deputies travelled to Versailles in May 1789, carrying the *cahiers de doléances* of the province with them, the country waited expectantly for the king to read and resolve their grievances. The Breton deputies who took part in the Estates General were particularly eager for reform, coming as they did from the third estate only; they were called the Grenadiers because of their strong stance against the powers of the court and the nobility. They kept in touch with their compatriots at home by corresponding with a network of committees based in reading clubs and literary chambers. Public readings of the deputies' letters, pamphlets and the newspaper *Le Héraut de la Nation*, founded in January 1789, meant that any Breton who was interested had the means of finding out about the latest political developments in Paris.

On 4 August 1789 the National Constituent Assembly, under the presidency of one of the Breton deputies, Le Chapelier, proclaimed the abolishment of all feudal rights. This proclamation unleashed a campaign of violence throughout France, dubbed *Le Grand Peur* (the Great Fear) as peasants descended on local noblemen demanding that they renounce their seigneurial rights. The reaction in Brittany was more moderate than in some areas but there were some flashpoints. For example the tenants of Laz and Trégourez descended on the castle of Spézet (*Speied*) in August, the abbey of Redon was pillaged and the peasants at Pontivy chased their local seigneur out of the parish. On the other hand, for example at Dol, there were instances where peasants intervened to protect their local castle from looters, although they themselves refused to pay the feudal taxes.

The succession of events left the Breton nobility bewildered and isolated. Some decided to bow down to the new order and took the civic oath that stripped them of their aristocratic rights.

About 30 per cent of them, mostly the very rich, chose exile in Jersey or London, while still others retired to their country houses where they kept a low profile, waiting to see what would happen next. Rumours of aristocratic plots led by exiled noblemen were rife that summer and the authorities reacted by taking control of the coastal fortifications and ensuring that sailors and soldiers located in Brittany were won over to the Revolution. The National Guards were also formed at this time. These were a series of local militias, usually urban, and their remit was to quell any royalist rebellion and peasant unrest in the countryside.

Some noblemen did indeed plan a comeback. One Armand Tuffin de la Rouerie, from the Fougères region, organized a counter-revolutionary movement called the Breton Association. He had the backing of the king's brothers and tried to extend the network of plotters into Normandy and Poitou as well. He urged the nobility to remain in Brittany and devised a network of committees throughout the province that were in constant touch with him. Some arms and ammunition were obtained. But the plot was discovered by the National Guard when they searched La Rouerie's castles in summer 1792 and he was executed in Rennes in October 1792.

When the Breton deputies participated in the vote to abolish aristocratic rights they also voted for the end of special privileges for Brittany. As most of these privileges had benefited the nobility in Brittany, rather than anyone else in the province, it seemed only right that these vestiges of the old feudal regime should be destroyed. The Breton estates and *parlement* were dismissed in November 1789. What the Breton deputies could not have realized at this stage was that the abolishment of Breton privileges was just the beginning of a process of centralization that would see the French state impose uniformity on every corner of the province, and intervene in the daily life of each citizen with an efficiency that was beyond the wildest dreams of even the most absolute monarch.

One very visible aspect of that centralization, that was put in place in winter 1789–90, was the creation of the *départements*. The old regions were swept away, to be replaced by administrative units that were meant to be roughly equal in area and population. Each *département* had an elected council and they took over the administrative tasks of the royal *intendants* and the policing powers of the *parlement*. The *département* was divided into districts and then again into communes, each with its own council and mayor. The aim of this measure was to create a single uniform system throughout France. Brittany's frontiers as a province were largely left intact as it now became five *départements*, Finistère, Côtes-du-Nord (Côtes-d'Armor today), Morbihan, Ille-et-Vilaine and Loire-Inférieure (Loire-Atlantique today). The dividing of the *départements* in Brittany was contentious with geographical, religious and linguistic borders largely ignored as the province was carved up into artificial units. Bitter rivalries appeared between towns as they vied for the prized position of being the seat of the local council. It has been argued that the final decisions on the borders were purely economic and made to satisfy the bourgeois lawyers and merchants of the province.

Indeed, it was the urban bourgeoisie who had led the Revolution in Brittany from the beginning, and it was they who benefited most. They dominated the municipal councils, often deliberately reducing rural representations by holding elections during harvest time, as Nantes did, and they fiercely protected their own rights as merchants and landowners. Thus, Nantes and Lorient opposed the abolition of slavery in February 1794, and the main bone of contention for many peasants in Brittany, the *domaine congéable* (a much hated system of a long lease tenancy), was not abolished immediately. In reality, the Revolution was an urban phenomenon created for the benefit of urban dwellers. The Enlightenment had not penetrated the rural masses and the town populations saw peasants as ignorant and illiterate people. The enmity of town and countryside was mutual, especially in times of food shortages (the harvest failed for the third time in summer 1789) when the towns could not understand that farmers needed to keep back some of their crops for the following year. Under the new regime the authorities were eager to ensure that the urban poor would not go hungry and they provided cheap bread while demanding that the agricultural hinterland provide them with it. The rural inhabitants were aghast at the grain flowing into the main centres of population like Brest and Nantes when they had hardly enough to feed themselves. Convoys of wheat travelling along the Loire were attacked, while 1,500 men had to be sent to Lannion (*Lannuon*) to recover 260 sacks of grain that were destined for Brest.

In fact, rural peasants had more and more reason to feel let down by the Revolution. Along with the grain, they were expected to provide men for military service as France's wars continued (members of the mostly urban National Guard were exempt) as well as horses and carts. Their feudal taxes were largely replaced by state taxes and the tenants were no better off under the bourgeois landlords. On top of this, many Breton communities found that some of their most fundamental traditions and beliefs came under attack when the Revolution began its systematic dismantling of the Church.

The initial onslaught on the Church started with the nationalization of its property and land in November 1789 followed by the prohibition of monastic vows in February 1790. Initially this was not seen too negatively by the local population. After all, many of the wealthy monasteries had exacted heavy taxes and some people actively supported this move; for example the Carmelites of Couëts, near Nantes, were publicly undressed and whipped by groups of local women. The religious boundaries were also redrawn with Brittany losing four of its original nine dioceses: Dol, Saint-Malo, Tréguier and Saint-Pol-de-Léon all disappeared. Bishops henceforth would be elected. This last move was welcomed by many parish priests who had taken part in the early days of the Revolution. Many a rural village had received the help of the local priest as they drew up their *cahiers* and several priests found themselves elected as mayors and municipal officers. The parish priest in Brittany, unlike some more anti-clerical areas of France, was very often a local man and he was known and respected in his community. When the Assembly insisted in November 1790 that every priest should take the oath to the Civil Constitution, many of these priests found themselves in a quandary. Several chose to give up their municipal post as they saw the Revolution following a path they could not follow, and the overwhelming majority of priests in Brittany refused to take the oath especially in Léon, Morbihan, pays de Redon, Vitré and along the border with the Vendée.

The non-juring priests were banished from the parish and some fled to Jersey or England. Many peasants were shocked by the way their local priest was treated. Several of them protested by presenting petitions of complaints and partaking in processions at night where they sang hymns and booed the oath-taking priests. Bishops were also supported; for example thousands of peasants converged on Vannes in February 1791 as they believed their bishop to be under threat. The National Guard, accompanied by four cannons, only dispersed them after a bloody confrontation that left ten dead. As opposition to the new religious laws increased the authorities reacted by imposing even harsher rules. The authorities of Côtes-du-Nord imprisoned the refractory priests in Dinan castle and allowed only one church per parish to remain open in January 1792. The other *départements* took similar measures as they crammed the non-compliant priests into prisons and exiled them to Spain and Jersey. The situation became particularly tense in the eastern districts of the province; for example in the October 1792 fair at Locmaria, in the district of Josselin, the crowd protested against the auction of the local monastery's property. Troops had to be called in and four peasants were killed, while one soldier was lynched by the mob.

Many parishes found themselves without a priest, while others had constitutional priests from other areas imposed on them. Unsurprisingly these men, who had taken the oath, were not welcomed by the congregation and troops were often used to ensure they could move into the presbytery safely. Meanwhile, the refractory priests often remained in the area, albeit in hiding, and they organized night processions, novenas and *pardons* to keep up the spirits of the faithful.

On the other hand, there were areas of Brittany that accepted the new religious administration without much protest. Indeed there were bands of anti-clerical territories in the Arrée mountains and the Carhaix basin and, along with the Fougères region, in the marshy regions of the pays de Retz and la Brière (*ar Briver*). In particular, in the centre of Finistère and south-west of Côtes-du-Nord, there was a group of about a hundred communes which were especially anti-clerical. They had suffered the yoke of the *quevaise*, a form of land tenancy to which they had been subjected by the abbeys of Bégard (*Bear*) and La Feuillée (*Ar Fouilhez*). Thus in these areas the refractory priests were not respected, as the non-jurors of La Guerche (*Ar Gwerc'h*) found when they were forced by the people to ride a donkey backwards.

There were some priests who had no difficulty with the taking of the constitutional oath. They were often urban based and intellectual like the teachers at the university of Nantes, and some likened the new order to a reform that echoed the simplicity of the early church. Both Brest and Lorient accepted constitutional priests, but not all towns did, with priests in Saint-Malo, Concarneau, Douarnenez and Vannes largely refraining from taking the oath.

While it may be argued that it was rural communities that gained least from the Revolution, life was not always rosy for the urban common people either. Rennes, Tréguier and Vannes all lost out economically as the estates and *parlement* no longer sat there. Brest, whose main industrial activity was naval construction, had gone into decline with the end of the American War, and Lorient suffered when the East Indies Company closed down in 1791. The tobacco factory at Morlaix also shut its doors in April 1791 and the following year just under half of the town's population were registered as paupers. The authorities were thus faced with possible unrest in the towns. They largely kept the social calm by providing cheap bread and Nantes practically bankrupted itself by following this policy. There were however incidents of urban popular dissent; for example there was a riot in Nantes in September 1792 as the price of bread rose too high despite the cautionary measures. Resentment of wealthy merchants, leading to one being brutally murdered by a mob, boiled over in Lorient in the same month. Brest saw demonstrations and strikes as many of the port workers found themselves unemployed or unpaid for months. Generally though, the authorities were able to keep the urban poor under control. The peasant uprising of 1793 however was another matter.

The spark that lit the violence was the command in February 1793 for 300,000 men to be conscripted into the French army. Each community had to provide a certain quota and so lots were drawn under the control of the mayor. This method had already caused riots in Lannion, Saint-Brieuc and Lamballe when it had been enforced the previous year, so when the order for even more men to be called up in this way was made the peasants were ready to erupt in anger. The revolt began at Fay (*Faouell*) in the district of Blain (*Blaen*) in the Loire-Inférieure on 10 March. It quickly spread, reaching Rennes on the 13th, Vannes on the 14th and north to Saint-Pol by the 19th. Towns like Clisson (*Klison*) were attacked and administrators were massacred as large groups of mostly young men ran from parish to parish, ringing the church bells to gather the people together and march on to the neighbouring towns. Things came to a head on 23 March when the commander of the troops stationed in Brittany met a crowd of several thousand peasants on the bridge of Kerguiduff between Saint-Pol and Lesneven. The ensuing battle left 300–400 dead, but Brest was saved from the peasant attacks and the rebellion was quashed. The region suffered repression as a result: the *département* of Finistère received a fine of 100,000 *livres*, the bell towers were pulled down, and the mayors of Ploudalmézeau (*Gwitalmeze*) and Plouzévéde (*Gwitevede*) were executed. There were other spontaneous insurrections further east at Redon and in the region of Saint-Brieuc that were also crushed, and order had more or less been established by April 1793.

The peasant unrest was not confined to Brittany; there were similar incidents in Maine, Anjou and Poitou as well. The 1793 uprising however did not develop into a general and organized movement such as the rebellion that was happening further south in the Vendée at the same time. There the counter-revolutionaries managed to mobilize a royalist army and posed a real threat to the Republic. The Vendée revolt touched the very south of Brittany when it reached the river Loire but, despite efforts to join up with the other Breton insurrectionists, the protests in the rest of the province were too localized and spontaneous for anything to come of them. These pockets of counter-revolutionary actions flared up again from time to time in different parts of Brittany and this kind of violence came to be known as *chouannerie* – the partakers being referred to as *chouans*. The origin of the name may come from the name of one of the local leaders, Jean Chouan, or may be a reference to the call of the owl which the rebels imitated when communicating with each other at night.

When the Vendée royalist army attacked Nantes in June the municipal authorities there called for help from the other Breton *départements*. Côtes-du-Nord sent a contingent of 600 men but the other *département* councils were more concerned with the threat from Paris as the radical Jacobins were taking control. More and more of the common people in Paris wanted the Revolution to go further than it had. They wanted a more egalitarian society and were willing to use violent means to achieve this. The Jacobin coup of June 1793 was a victory for people power. Robespierre took hold of the reins and the Terror began. This phase of the Revolution was very much a Parisian phenomenon and the reforms had to be imposed on the provinces.

There were some Jacobin supporters in Brittany although they were few in number and had little influence on the majority. There was a network of clubs and societies of friends of the Constitution that were affiliated to the Jacobin clubs in Paris. Indeed there were forty-three such clubs in Brittany at the beginning of 1792 and almost every town of any size had one. This is not to say, however, that they necessarily agreed completely with the ultra-radical factions of Paris, but rather that they were favourable to the Revolution as they saw it.

In general the men who controlled the councils in Brittany were urban bourgeoisie who felt that the Revolution had gone far enough. In the beginning they had identified with Paris, but they had also identified with other provincial cities and had created so-called federations of like-minded urban centres. For example, the representatives of 129 town councils met in Morlaix in February 1790 in order to combine their efforts to calm the peasant unrest. These federations of local town councils, which were created all over provincial France, were in no way anti-Paris or seeking regional autonomy; rather they glorified in the diversity of the regions that had benefited from the Revolution as one. However, the paranoid Jacobin authorities now saw all manifestations of federalism as a threat. In addition to this, the majority of the Breton deputies in Paris supported the opposing Gironde faction and they had often complained about the increasingly bloodthirsty politics of the capital. Their hostility increased after the death of king Louis XVI in January 1793. Of the forty-three Breton deputies present in government in Paris at the time, only fourteen voted for his execution. So when the Jacobins gained power in June, any difference of opinion, any regional aspect, was treated as treason. Breton deputies such as Kervélégan and Gomaire from Finistère were arrested, and many municipal counsellors and mayors in Brittany found themselves heading for the guillotine. The popular societies inspired by federalism were 'reformed' and elected administrators were replaced by named national agents. Ten-day reports to Paris were demanded from each council and revolutionary tribunals were set up in each *département* to try those suspected of treason. The Jacobins felt that they were fighting an enemy within as well as the foreign wars.

The threat of federalism was real. In late June 1793 the general council of Finistère called on the Breton communes to meet in Rennes where they decided to raise some troops in collaboration with communes in Normandy. However the action was poorly prepared and badly led and the rebels were routed at Pacy-sur-Eure on 13 July. Finistère paid dearly for its role in this federalist revolt. The twenty-six administrators of the *département* were executed, including the bishop of Quimper and the mayor of Brest.

Purging local councils of dissenting administrators however was not enough for the Jacobin authorities. They sent in deputies-on-mission with special far-reaching powers to make sure that the new rules were enforced. These men were sent all over France but Brittany suffered from especially sadistic and cruel ones who virtually had a free rein to do what they wanted. Only Côtes-du-Nord did not suffer this treatment, probably because the *département* had not contributed to the federalist revolt or been subjected to *chouan* unrest. Apart from a few local Jacobin clubs most of the population were uncooperative and troops had to be sent in to drive the point home.

One thing that the anti-clerical Jacobins truly despised was the Catholic church, and not satisfied with having stripped it of its wealth and banishing non-constitutional priests it now decided to ban religion altogether. Churches were closed down, cathedrals were sacked and crosses and calvaries were mutilated. The revolutionary calendar did away with Sunday and even the priests and bishops who had taken the constitutional oath found themselves persecuted. The relish with which the Jacobins attacked the church and their absolute contempt for believers is exemplified by the commissioner Dragon's behaviour in Quimper. On 13 December 1793, which was the feast day of the town's patron saint, Saint Corentin, he destroyed the statues and ornaments in the cathedral and then publicly urinated in a ciborium.

Several refractory priests were imprisoned and executed between 1793 and 1796 including the infamous case of the 843 who were drowned in the river Loire by being chained to barges that were then scuttled. This was the work of the deputy-on-mission Jean-Baptiste Carrier who also shot another fifty priests. All the *départements* in Brittany saw executions during the Terror but while the numbers of victims were usually in the hundreds, the figure for Nantes was in the thousands. Carrier was responsible for shooting about 3,000, between 2,000 and 5,000 were drowned and another 3,000 starved to death in the prisons. These figures are among the highest for the whole of France. Even Robespierre deemed Carrier excessive and called him back to Paris. The victims of these executions, as well as the priests, were royalists, federalists and the wealthy, but most of all they were rebellious peasants as *chouannerie* actions were never totally absent.

The causes of the uprising in March 1793 had not disappeared and with the repression the tensions only worsened. From autumn 1793 onwards however the *chouans* changed their tactics. No longer attacking towns and attempting pitched battles they acted in small mobile bands practising guerrilla tactics that were well suited to the Breton *bocage* landscape of small fields and pastures enclosed by thick hedgerows. The protagonists were no longer exclusively rural peasants; they now included unemployed textile workers, beggars, republican deserters and others who had no wish to be conscripted. Among them were plain bandits and ex-salt smugglers who had lost their way of life when France's internal borders and customs were swept away by the Revolution. These were hardened, well-armed men from the very poorest of society and had nothing to lose. They operated mainly by night, launching surprise attacks and creating a climate of fear by assassinating well-known Jacobin supporters. They consisted of several different groups each with their own local leader such as Guillemot in Bignan (*Begnen*) region and Cadoudal who operated close to Auray. Even some old allies of La Rouerie reappeared like Boishardy in the region of Lamballe. The sporadic and scattered nature of the insurrection made it very difficult for the authorities to quell it. One method was to send in mobile columns of armies that punished the rebellious regions by killing indiscriminately. General Hoche attempted a different tactic by signing a truce with various counter-revolutionary leaders at the castle of La Prévalaye, south-west of Rennes, in April 1795. But the truce did not last and after some of the main leaders were arrested the *chouans* in the Morbihan attacked the gunpowder factory of Pont-de-Buis in June. Ten days later, between 8,000 and 9,000 men led by Count Puisaye and others appeared on the Quiberon peninsula where they met a group of aristocratic exiles who landed accompanied by British troops. However the operation had been badly planned and some of the *chouans* refused to fight. Hoche arrived with his troops, blocked off the peninsula, and took 6,000 prisoners.

When the Jacobins were overthrown in July 1794, Brittany, along with the rest of the provinces, heaved a sigh of relief. There now took place the trials and executions of prominent Jacobin terrorists, including that of Carrier, who was probably the most infamous of them all. In February 1795 religion was permitted once more and the distrustful refractory priests came out of hiding. They had to declare their submission to the Republic, however, before they were allowed to use some churches again. Many took this compromise oath but, once again, hardly any succumbed to this in the Morbihan. Another deputy-on-mission, Boursault, was sent to Brittany, but he was a reasonable man and he was accompanied by two Breton assistants. He engineered the release of many prisoners, including some Girondin ex-administrators and the Jacobin clubs in the province were encouraged to dwindle away as their correspondence network was forbidden.

The new government, however, was concerned about the possible growing support for Royalists and there was a return to Jacobin methods of control after September 1797. The councils were purged once more, elections were cancelled and the non-juring priests were persecuted again. This time it was the Côtes-du-Nord that was most affected as eighteen clerics were beaten and nearly fifty were imprisoned or deported. Only one priest was executed though, at Saint-Brieuc. The churches were turned into Theophilanthropic temples and the authorities tried their best to make the people recognize the *décadi*, the tenth day of the revolutionary week, as the day of worship.

Predictably *chouannerie* erupted again as a result of the renewed religious persecution and repression. *Chouans* raided Saint-Brieuc and Nantes and freed all the prisoners. Constitutional priests were attacked including the bishop of Quimper who was murdered. All of the countryside of Ille-et-Vilaine was under the control of the *chouans* during this period and it is estimated that there were about 10,000 active *chouans* in Brittany in 1799. As a counter-revolutionary movement *chouannerie* expressed all the elements of the Revolution that had left the people dissatisfied. Religious repression, taxes and conscription were all factors, exacerbated by failed harvests and inflation; but although there were aristocrats among the *chouans* it is unlikely that the bulk of the peasants wanted the return of the *ancien régime* and feudalism. Nor was it confined to either Breton or French-speaking areas but rather flared up regularly in both Lower and Upper Brittany.

In November 1799 Napoleon Bonaparte seized power and proclaimed himself First Consul, and the people, exhausted by civil as well as foreign wars, hoped that this military general could bring some stability to the country. Napoleon was concerned with reinforcing the central authority of Paris over rebellious provinces and he suspended the constitution in ten *départements* that included the Morbihan, Côtes-du-Nord, Ille-et-Vilaine and Loire-Inférieure. The local town councils lost much of their control as the consul appointed prefects, men from outside Brittany who were much more powerful than the old *intendants* and directly accountable to Paris. Napoleon viewed Brittany with suspicion as a nest of counter-revolutionaries and he moved the garrison from Rennes to be based at Pontivy, right in the middle of *chouan* country. He also planned to build a new military town there, on the plan of La Roche-sur-Yon in the Vendée, so that the army could easily suppress any discontent. By 1815 however only the roads and the essential buildings had been completed.

Napoleon also created secondary schools and faculties in Rennes, Nantes and Pontivy. There was no question that education should reflect the local region in any way, either linguistically or otherwise; rather, the education was meant to form and control a francophone elite which could function anywhere in France.

One move that was welcomed by many Bretons was the re-authorization of public worship on a Sunday. The constitutional priests were released and the refractory ones allowed to return. After the long years of persecution most were willing to conform to the Concordat of April 1802 that firmly placed the clergy within the state. Only a tiny group refused to cooperate this time. They still felt loyalty to the pre-1789 bishops who were still alive and together they formed the 'little church'. The new bishops were not elected, however, but appointed by the state and they were all non-Breton loyal Bonapartistes. They in turn were supposed to choose priests who would preach that paying taxes and doing military service was the duty of all good Christians. The civil and religious authorities did not always see eye to eye on the choice of priests as many bishops actually preferred the refractory priests. Some peasants were quickly trained to make up the numbers as the average age for the depleted priesthood was fifty, but they were not always of the best quality.

Chouannerie reduced in importance fairly quickly after the rise of Napoleon. There was still the occasional dramatic incident, like the assassination of the constitutional bishop of Finistère in 1800, but gradually the roaming bands that still remained were caught and one by one the leaders were captured and executed, or fled the country as Cadoudal did. He was involved in the 1803 plot against Napoleon. From 1802 the *chouans* were no longer a real problem but they could still pose a threat, as the kidnapping of the Bonapartiste bishop of Vannes in 1806 showed. Areas in Upper Brittany and Morbihan, especially after 1808, had their share of draft dodgers who hid in clandestine groups. There was a brief resurgence of *chouannerie* in 1815 during Napoleon's first fall from grace, and 12,000 soldiers were needed to control the uprising in the pays de Guérande.

Napoleon was a military dictator and France had been at war, more or less constantly, since 1792. The war that affected Brittany most was the one with Great Britain, which altogether lasted twenty-three years. However, because of the government's preoccupation with the north-eastern frontiers, rather than developing its strategic offensive possibilities, Brittany found itself in a defensive position. The province suffered blockades as the British navy controlled the entrances to the bays of Saint-Brieuc and Douarnenez and even the Loire estuary. Indeed, other than the pirate ships of Saint-Malo that captured 170 enemy ships between 1803 and 1813, hardly any boat dared venture out further than ten miles from the coast. In 1800 the blockade prevented the French fleet from leaving Brest harbour and Napoleon's brother's ship, the *Vétéran*, was blocked in the port of Concarneau for three years. But Napoleon was not interested in developing marine infrastructure in Brittany, the way he did in Cherbourg and Anvers. The military port created at Saint-Servan in 1801 was abandoned in 1804 and port workers at Brest and Lorient found themselves redundant.

The war affected trade and commerce as goods were no longer imported or exported and agriculture suffered from a shortage of manpower as thousands of peasants left to fight. Port traffic in Nantes dropped by 84 per cent from 1792–1807, and the number of workers involved in manufacturing in Loire-Inférieure dropped from 23,000 to 16,000. Textile workers in general decreased in number, mines collapsed and even the salt marshes were in crisis.

Brittany in 1815 was a society that had suffered economic disaster and social upheaval. It had lost all vestige of local autonomy and the people were deeply divided into Whites (anti-revolution and Catholic) and Blues (republican and secular). Its relationship with France had been changed profoundly by the Revolution and Napoleon's reign. Administratively it no longer existed, and it had earned the reputation of being backward, reactionary and obscure, shackled by its superstitious Catholicism and Breton language.

8

Emigration, religion and language (1815–1914)

Brittany in the nineteenth century was in many ways a rural backwater with an under-developed industrial infrastructure whose economy could not cope with the rise in population. The advent of the railways made Brittany more accessible than it had ever been and while the trains brought in tourists, ever eager to witness the stunning rugged scenery and quaint old-fashioned people, the railway carriages also transported emigrants who were leaving the province, desperate for a better life. The century which saw the holiday industry in Brittany really begin to develop also saw thousands of Bretons leaving the province in droves. The majority of those who left never gave a thought to their native language as they sought their fortunes in Paris and other French-speaking cities; and yet this is also the century that saw the germination of interest in Breton language and culture that was ultimately to lead, in certain circles, to nationalist sentiments.

Most of those who left were escaping rural poverty as unemployment forced many into destitution, exacerbated by the high rate of alcoholism. Beggars were part of the landscape, as early twentieth-century postcards testify, and in 1847–8 over 18,500 people died of starvation in Lower Brittany. Some inland areas were left almost deserted as people flocked to the cities. Many ended up as domestic servants in Rennes and Paris while others sought more fertile lands where they could continue as agricultural labourers. Men who had found work when the railways were first built then left with the trains, and conscripts who had been garrisoned in the east did not return. By 1911 400,000 Bretons, almost 12 per cent of the population, lived outside the peninsula. Some Bretons overcame their poverty with seasonal migration to places such as the Channel Islands while the turn of the twentieth century saw the appearance of the enterprising Onion Johnnies, or *Sioni Winwns* as they were called by the Welsh, who sailed from Roscoff with bicycles laden with vegetables that they could sell for twice the price in the south of England and Wales.

The main reason for Brittany's poverty was the increase in population; the birth rate here was higher than anywhere else in France. From 2,200,000 in 1801 Brittany's population in 1911 was 3,270,000. The mainly agricultural economy of the province could not provide for this number of people. Although new agricultural techniques began to penetrate in the second half of the nineteenth century any new methods were adopted at a very slow and gradual pace. The cultivation of rye and barley gradually decreased and a new crop was introduced, the potato. Some areas such as Trégor and Léon were able to produce enough vegetables to export via Roscoff. The farms slowly became mechanized and the railways and canals brought in much needed fertilizers such as guano from Peru and *noir* which was a waste product from the sugar refineries in Nantes. Another new crop was rape, and the rearing of cows also increased. The polycultural nature of Breton agriculture was to show its advantages at the end of the century when the region managed to avoid the disasters that hit the monocultural grain and vine regions of France. In fact, by 1914, Brittany was one of the most important agricultural regions in France, producing a quarter of its horses, 14 per cent of its cattle, 10 per cent of its pigs and large quantities of vegetables and cereals. Nevertheless, it was the landowners who benefited most from this agricultural wealth, the rural salaries here were the lowest in France.

Many of the rural emigrants went seeking work in Nantes, the main commercial centre of Brittany, and the city and its suburbs grew from 74,000 in 1801 to nearly 200,000 by the following century. The port continued to develop its economic activities during the nineteenth century and this included recreating its lucrative slave trade when slavery was reintroduced by Napoleon in 1802. The trade was finally made illegal in 1827. The pre-Revolutionary activity of sugar refining continued success-fully until the competition from sugar beet and refineries in the north of France became too much in the 1880s. Nantes' main success story though was the Lefèvre-Utile biscuit factories. There were four of these, employing 1,000 workers, and in 1900 they produced 4,500,000 tonnes of biscuits. Ship building was still important here and in 1913 it had four major naval construction sites; its main rival now was Saint-Nazaire which had been chosen in 1861 to be the centre for building iron ships. This port, a fishing village in 1800, gained 19,000 inhabitants by 1868.

The lower Loire region also supported cokeworks and the arsenal at Indret employed over 2,000 workers during the Crimean War. The other arsenals at Brest, Lorient and Rennes and the gunpowder factories of Pont-de-Buis (*Pont-ar-Veuzenn*) and Relecq-Kerhuon (*Releg-Kerhuon*) all profited when France was at war.

One of Brittany's traditional industries, fishing, underwent a major development when canning was invented in 1810. Sardine fishing came into its own as tonnes of fish were conserved in canning factories in Nantes and other coastal towns such as Concarneau, Douarnenez and Audierne. At one point Brittany was responsible for nearly 90 per cent of the world production in tinned sardines. The industry received a blow in the 1880s when rival canning factories, run by Breton businessmen, were set up in Spain and Portugal where labour was cheaper, the olive oil local and the sardines just as plentiful. Another knock was the introduction of soldering machines which replaced the need for skilled male workers. At its peak the sardine canning industry in Brittany employed 15,000 workers, most of whom were female.

While sardines dominated the southern coast the north coast continued to fish for cod off Newfoundland. The fishermen of the nineteenth century also ventured regularly up to Greenland and Iceland; for example the port of Paimpol (*Pempoull*) sent seventy-four boats there in 1895. However, the industry began to decline as fresh cod, transported directly to the cities by trains, competed with their salted cod. The 1905 treaty with Britain, which excluded French fishing boats from certain sections of the Canadian coast, merely exacerbated the situation. Only Saint-Malo remained as a major cod fishing port by the twentieth century.

Another of Brittany's traditional industries, textiles, had all but disappeared by the end of the nineteenth century. Initially, the industry recovered after the chaos of the Revolution and the Empire and by 1820 the number of textile workers in the Loudéac (*Loudieg*) district had increased to 4,000. Several small textile workshops appeared in Trégor where a simple and cheap machine, well adapted to small watermills, was in use. Half the textiles produced in Léon were sent to Brest to be made into sails. By the mid-century though the industry was facing competition from northern France, especially Picardy, where more advanced mechanical spinning mills were being used. In addition cheap cotton was fast becoming the fashionable material for clothes and to top it all the new steam ships being built had no need for sails. Of the 9,623 weavers employed in northern Brittany in 1825, only 1,637 remained thirty years later. The textile association of Léon closed its doors in 1891. A few workshops in Trégor survived until the 1950s. One former textile town succeeded in adapting admirably by reinventing itself as the shoe capital of France. Fougères by 1890 had twenty-seven shoe factories which employed 11,000 workers.

The factories of Fougères were the exception. The vast majority of the industrial establishments, outside the industrialized south-east, employed fewer than five people. Lacking in natural mineral resources, such as coal, and suffering from under investment, most of Brittany was on the periphery of the modern industrial world.

The emigrants who left Brittany or simply moved to the towns seeking employment very often abandoned their native language altogether. Anybody who wanted to improve his lot needed to know French, and Breton and Gallo (a Romance language spoken in the east of the country) were increasingly perceived as the languages of the illiterate peasant. Both languages were banned from use in the classrooms and schoolyard and teachers were fined and pupils punished if they were caught speaking it. In 1837, for example, Guillaume Marzel, a primary school teacher at Saint-Renan, was heavily fined for teaching written Breton to his pupils. From 1885 onwards there was a system similar to the 'Welsh Not' in operation. This consisted of making a child who had been caught speaking Breton or Gallo wear around his neck an object, called the *symbole* or *vache*. The guilty child was then encouraged to listen out for other offenders so that the *symbole* would be passed on to the next one. The pupil caught with the *symbole* at the end of the day would be punished as well as humiliated. None of the parents objected particularly to this policy as they saw that their children needed to learn French properly. The negative attitude towards Breton in particular did not come simply from Paris; the sub-prefect of Finistère in 1845 declared to the local teachers 'Above all, remember Sirs, that you have been appointed to kill the Breton language.'

Despite the persecution the linguistic frontier that divided Breton and non-Breton speaking Brittany hardly changed between 1806 and 1886. The only real decline was in the coastal areas, especially in south Morbihan. Rather, the result of the language policy was to make the lower classes bilingual as they spoke Breton at home and in church but French in school and in town.

The church became an ally of the Breton language during the nineteenth century. It had long followed the policy of encouraging priests to communicate with their congregations in their own language, but it now saw that the Breton language could be a useful tool in the battle against secularism. Many priests had seen first-hand how the rural peasant, once he had moved to the town or city, abandoned both his faith and his language. The French language thus came to be considered as the vehicle by which secular values and immoral ideas were conveyed and so it was argued that the promotion of the Breton language and culture would also defend the Catholic faith. It was in this spirit that the Breton language religious journal *Feiz ha Breiz* (Faith and Brittany) was launched in 1865, with the official support of the bishop of Quimper, and that Breton lessons were given at the seminary in Vannes and in the college of Saint-Charles in Saint-Brieuc. In 1905 the association *Bleun-Brug* (heather flowers) was launched by the priest Yann-Vari Perrot with the aim of fostering Catholic values along with Breton culture and language.

Secularism and indifference were not the only dangers to the church; laws decreed from Paris were also a threat. Until 1833 nearly all the schools in Brittany were run either by the local parish priest or by a religious order, for example the Christian Brothers of Ploërmel (*Ploermael*) managed 353 schools in 1879. But many isolated areas had no school whatsoever and illiteracy was high in Brittany. The Guizot law of 1833 obliged every commune to have a primary school, and the teachers for these new schools were trained in teacher-training colleges. These colleges quickly developed into anti-clerical seminaries, although religious instruction had originally been on the syllabus. These schools now competed with the existing religious schools in certain areas. The first of the Jules Ferry laws of the 1880s attempted to diminish the influence of the religious schools by forbidding certain orders such as the Jesuits and Capucins from teaching and managing such schools. In 1882 primary education was made compulsory and religious instruction was only allowed, if the parents saw fit, outside the school building. Priests were no longer allowed to enter the school to give catechism and from 1887 religious instruction was only allowed outside school hours. In 1901 the government closed down any school that was still being run by a religious order, and the Emile Combes law of 1903 extended this to include all Catholic schools. Combes's law also forbade giving catechism and sermons in Breton in church, which only served to convince the church that the Breton language and the faith were inextricably linked. Many priests in the diocese of Quimper, supported by the bishop, lost their salaries for the offence of using Breton in their church.

The order to close down church schools and expel religious orders met with resistance in Brittany in both Breton and non-Breton speaking areas. The clerics and parents who defended the schools in Saint-Méen (*Sant-Neven*) and le Folgoët (*Ar*

Folgoad) had to be dispersed by police. The municipal council voted against the dissolution of the Christian Brothers of Ploërmel and were angered when they were overridden by Paris. The local paper, *Le Ploëmelais*, launched a press campaign against this 'legal burglary'. In the end, the government sent an army of 1,200 men in February 1904 to evacuate the brothers on the designated date of their dissolution. This included moving old and sick people out of their hospice. When the authorities moved on to close the school they found the building barricaded by the local people in protest. The brothers of Ploërmel subsequently moved their mother house to Taunton, Somerset.

The law separating the church and state in 1905 and the inventorying of church property in 1906 heightened the tensions in many parts of Brittany. Clergy and faithful acted together to try and prevent state officials from assessing the value of the churches. In some localities the churches were transformed into fortresses where the police were bombarded with stones; in other places congregations dug ditches, built barricades and burnt sulphur in their attempts to protect their church. Thus the officials were severely hampered in their work as, for example, in the Côtes-du-Nord, only 170 inventories were drawn up out of 403.

The lengths that Breton parishioners were willing to go to protect their church demonstrates how the church had succeeded to survive and regenerate itself after the persecution and suppression of the Revolution and the chaos of the Empire. Although there were areas of Brittany that were downright anti-clerical it is estimated that 75 per cent of all Bretons in the nineteenth century, whatever their political opinion, still attended the Easter mass. The first problem that the church faced was a deficiency of priests and this was tackled by ordaining hundreds of new priests; Brittany became a veritable clerical factory as Breton seminaries churned out thousands of priests. Many of these went abroad on missions or helped to fill empty places in areas of France lacking a priest. The social class of the recruits was different from that of before the Revolution as 60 per cent of the Breton clergy in the nineteenth century were of lower or middle peasant origin.

Another problem that faced the church in the early nineteenth century was that many of the faithful had reverted to traditions that bordered on the superstitious, due to the lack of guidance from a parish priest. This was solved by missionaries descending on parishes from time to time. They came in groups of thirty or forty priests and attempted to shock the faithful back on to the narrow path with dramatic sermons preaching austerity and eternal damnation, using graphic images such as skulls and *taolennoù* (pictures) to drive the point home. One of the most prominent missionaries was Jean-Marie de Lamennais, founder of the Christian Brothers at Ploërmel. They were not always welcome however; for example they received short shrift from the sailors of Brest.

Calvaries and crosses that had been destroyed during the Revolution were rebuilt, and several new churches were constructed, being often very large in order to accommodate the increasing population. Many church buildings had been closed for several years, or had been used as storehouses, and they were in a sorry state. In 1802 in the Morbihan there were thirty-three churches in ruins and eighty-six needed major repairs. Thanks to donations, voluntary work, and public funds many of these churches were rebuilt or repaired. The building pace gathered speed in the second half of the century as ninety churches were reconstructed in Finistère, ninety-five in Loire-Inférieure and a hundred in the Morbihan. Not since the Middle Ages had Brittany seen such a frenzy of church building. The new churches often bore no resemblance to their medieval predecessors but rather were in the neo-classical or neo-Gothic style. Many were massive impressive granite constructions as the church attempted to compete with the symbols of secularism in the form of the new public buildings such as railway stations and town halls.

The annual *pardons* and pilgrimages were as popular as ever and the newly built railway system enabled enormous crowds to gather from the middle of the century onwards. Forty thousand went to the *pardon* of Notre-Dame-du-Folgoët in 1873, and 60,000 attended in 1888. The most popular site was Sainte-Anne-d'Auray (*Santez-Anna-Wened*), where an enormous basilica was built in 1864.

Colourful *pardons* and devout peasants in traditional dress all added to the romantic image of Brittany in the nineteenth century and which attracted visitors here. Enchanted by quaint old-fashioned ways and megalithic monuments Brittany became a fashionable curiosity for authors such as Balzac, Flaubert and Stendhal. Artists, including Turner who visited here in 1826, also found the rugged scenery and picturesque people alluring and painters like Corot, Renoir, and Gaugin flocked here. They painted scenes of Cancale (*Kankaven*), Concarneau and Douarnenez while Pont-Aven became an artist's colony where the inhabitants were quite used to posing as models. Indeed, in 1890, Gaugin grumbled that Pont-Aven had become too much of a tourist trap and he moved on to Pouldu in search of authenticity. The popularity of Brittany as a holiday destination increased in the last decades of the century and the railways facilitated the journey for many who simply wanted to enjoy the coast. Bathing was becoming popular, a hydrotherapy centre was set up in Le Croisic (*Ar Groazig*) in 1859 and summer villas sprung up all along the sea-front in places like Dinard (*Dinarzh*) and Perros-Guirec (*Perroz-Gireg*). La Baule (*Ar Baol*), founded in 1876, was the most popular resort in 1900 while Pornichet (*Pornizhan*) could count 500 villas, ten hotels and a casino among its attractions in the same year.

While visitors came to enjoy and admire the countryside there were those within Brittany who began to display an interest in the language, history and culture of the country. Le Gonidec (1775–1838), a minor nobleman who was a civil servant from Le Conquet (*Konk-Leon*), published a Breton grammar in 1807 and a Breton–French dictionary in 1821. His scholarly works were the basis of a standard orthography for modern Breton. Those who wished to know more about the history of the land could read Arthur de La Borderie's (1827–1901) three-volumed *Histoire de Bretagne* published between 1896 and 1899. Some scholars realized that there were cultural gems to be had in the country's oral literature and people like Count Kergariou (1776–1849) and Jean Marie de Penguern (1807–56) toured the countryside collecting folk tales and songs. François-Marie Luzel

(1821–95) was another avid collector and he published five volumes of folktales and four volumes of songs. The most famous collector of Breton folk songs was Théodore Hersart de La Villemarqué (1815–95) who first published the *Barzaz Breiz* in 1839. This collection of folk ballads, edited and translated by La Villemarqué, accompanied by copious notes, took the literary world by storm. The book appeared at a time when the romantic vogue was at its height in Europe and it was well received by the milieu that had been delighted by McPherson's *Ossian*. In the subsequent years countless authors would cite the *Barzaz Breiz* as the book that had inspired them to compose literature in Breton, or simply to learn the language for themselves.

This interest among erudites in the language and history of Brittany was echoed by similar movements in other provinces in France as they struggled to define their identity in the new post-Revolutionary France. A number of the savants who were key figures in the movement were of noble origin, and some of the interest was partly due to nostalgia for the ways things were under the *ancien régime*. Various Celtic and archaeological societies were founded and a new pride in Bretonness developed in certain circles. Most of the gatherings were purely cultural but there were some who began to chafe at the suppression, as they saw it, of the Breton people by France. One example of this repression that was often quoted was the massacre of Conlie.

In 1870, while France was at war with the Prussians, the prefect of police Kerartry, who was the deputy for Finistère, was ordered by the government to form a 'Breton army'. He assembled about 60,000 men at Conlie, 25 km from Le Mans, and proceeded to give them military instruction. But the government was overcome by fear that this Breton battalion could be harbouring *chouan* sentiments and become a rebellious army so it was decided not to supply the men with weapons. The Bretons were also left to winter at Conlie despite the inadequate supplies and many fell ill. When the Prussians invaded France and fought the battle of Le Mans in January 1871 the under-armed and unprepared Breton troops were slaughtered.

Although events like Conlie could provoke indignation and bitterness the early Breton associations (now referred to collectively as the first *Emsav*) were not particularly political. The URB (*l'Union Régionaliste Bretonne*) founded in 1898 included members like Anatole Le Braz, who published folk songs and legends; but in 1911 a splinter group formed the FRB (*la Fédération Régionaliste de Bretagne*) as they deemed the URB to be too conservative. The FRB began to show an interest in the economy of Brittany but it was the PNB (*le Parti Nationaliste Breton*), also founded in 1911, which first espoused political ideas. There were vague calls for independence and the party protested vehemently against the monument in Rennes, erected in 1910, which celebrated the union of Brittany with France. But the PNB did not have any clear political policies. It would take the experience of the First World War to spawn a new generation of true nationalists.

Plate 1. Gallo-Roman temple at Fanum Martis (modern day Corseul), capital of the Coriosolitae tribe.

Plate 2. Close-up of the Roman temple wall at Corseul.

Plate 3. Statute at Nominoé at Bains-sur-Oust. He was the first Breton duk
and was victorious at the battle of Ballon 845 when he defeated the Frankish
king Charles the Bald.

Plate 4. Medieval street in Dinan. Dinan was one of the medium sized urban centres that developed during the fourteenth century in Brittany.

Plate 5. Twelfth century bell tower of the abbey of Saint-Sauveur de Redon. Founded in 832 by Conwoion this was an important cultural and ecclesiastical centre.

Plate 6. Ducal castle at Suscinio. Inset – 14th century tiled floor from the castle's extramural chapel.

Plate 7. Many calvary crosses were destroyed during the French Revolution. Some, like this sixteenth century one at Guéhenno, were subsequently restored during the nineteenth century religious resurgence.

Plate 8. The elaborately carved façade of St Armel church in Ploërmel testifies to the prosperity that Brittany experienced during its Golden Age (mid sixteenth to mid seventeenth century).

Plate 9. Birth house of the peasant chouan leader Pierre Guillemot at Kerdel (near Bignan). Recently restored by the Association Pierre Guillemot this is a typical late eighteenth century Morbihan farmhouse.

Plate 10. Late nineteenth century summer villa in the tourist resort of Dinard.

Plate 11. National Monument to the Breton victims, both civilian and military, of the First World War at Ste-Anne-d'Auray. This site was chosen because of its national importance as a centre of pilgrimage.

Plate 12. Detail of frieze by Le Bozex showing war victims.

9

From the Great War to the eve of the Second World War (1914–39)

The physical and psychological scars that the Great War left on Brittany were profound. The numbers of those from Brittany who were killed were high, greater than the average for France, and so many women wore mourning black for the rest of their lives that the colourful nature of the traditional dress was almost forgotten. For those men who survived, the experience of life in the French army and exposure to new places caused many to consider Brittany hereafter in a new light.

The estimated number of those who died in the First World War has varied wildly but today the accepted figure is about 120,000. Brittany's contribution in manpower was higher than many other areas of France due to its rural nature; the peasant farmer was deemed easier to replace than the skilled worker who was needed to keep the factories running. Thus it was the women, children and older men who had to try and maintain Breton agriculture. Yet, ironically, for some the war was a financial bonus. The front line was far away and the country itself did not suffer from any battles, so for many the main hardship was the absence of their menfolk. The government provided an allowance for soldiers' families, and in the poorest most backward farms in the province this allowance was greater than the living they managed to eke out during peace time. The price of basic commodities rose sharply here as elsewhere, causing real privation to many, but those farmers who were responsible for providing some of those basic products, such as eggs and butter, found their profits increasing beyond anything they had experienced before. For the lucky ones this meant being able to pay off their chronic debts for the first time ever and some peasant farmers were able to buy their own land. However, whether this made up for the sacrifice of their sons is debatable.

Breton industry was also affected by the war. The factories redirected their energies into the war effort: the Basse-Indre steelworks, for example, manufactured shells and the naval yards at Nantes were transformed into munitions factories. The canneries were vital in the effort to ensure food supplies for the army and shoe production at Fougères now consisted of thousands of military boots. The arsenals of Brest, Lorient and Rennes increased their usual production of ammunition and war materials. Yet most of the regular workforce had been mobilized to the front, so it was mostly women who worked the machines, even in the foundries. The rest of the shortfall was made up by foreign refugees and German prisoners of war.

Although the Breton factory workers had guaranteed work and a regular wage during the war, the wages were constantly being eroded by the rising prices, especially in basic foodstuffs like sugar, potatoes, rice and butter. Consequently in the spring and summer of 1917 a series of strikes broke out, involving some 5,000 women and 1,500 men at the arsenal and gas factory in Rennes and 2,500 women downed tools in the powder works of Pont-de-Buis, supported by the women in the sardine factory at Audierne. The arsenal at Brest and the naval workers of Saint-Nazaire also joined in. These were protests at the difficult living conditions rather than a demonstration of any anti-war feelings, and although the people, like everywhere else, were tired of the length of the war, Brittany, on the whole, supported the war.

Brittany also welcomed scores of allied troops as they passed through the ports on their way to the front. Brest received 30,000 Russians, Canadians and Portuguese along with some 800,000 Americans. The main naval base was Saint-Nazaire where 120,000 British troops were stationed in August 1914, and this was where the Americans built camps, hangars, a hospital and a landing stage at Montoir (Mouster-al-Loc'h). The port activity was such that Saint-Nazaire became the fifth most important port in France.

As for the men who were mobilized into the army, the Breton-speaking peasants among them in particular experienced a profound cultural shock. As well as suffering the horrors of the trenches and warfare, they found themselves treated with contempt by their superiors because of their poor or non-existent French and their apparent backwardness. There are anecdotes of Breton soldiers being shot because of misunderstandings, not helped by the fact that the Breton and German word for 'yes' sound the same. They also had opportunities to experience for themselves how primitive their own farms were. While marching to the front they saw farmsteads with electricity and running water, luxuries not thought of at home. They compared notes with soldiers from urban backgrounds and heard of a better life in the towns. Many of those who survived the war never went back to Brittany, while others returned only to collect their families and move on to seek a higher quality of life in the town. Most of those who did go back and stay swore that they would not allow their children to suffer the indignities they had suffered, and they made a conscious effort not to pass the Breton language on to their offspring. Thus the First World War had a detrimental effect on the Breton language and accelerated the pace of emigration. From 1911–21 people left rural Brittany at the rate of about 17,000 a year. The exodus then slowed down somewhat but continued between 1921 and 1935 when the annual rate was 11,500. It was not only ex-soldiers and their families who left; a high proportion of the emigrants were young women.

The First World War also marks a new phase in the Breton movement as members of the so-called second *Emsav* developed more definite political ideas. Some of the younger members of the pre-war movement, such as the poet Bleimor (Yann-Ber Kalloc'h) and writer Dirlemm (Joseph Pierre Le Bras), had died in battle and a new generation of young men came to take their place. Their experience of war had served to reinforce their Breton identity and made them determined to create a new Brittany after the war. Impatient with the nostalgic ideology of the URB and FRB (see previous chapter) and inspired by the Irish uprising of Easter 1916 the young, idealistic leaders tended to be from Upper Brittany and had learned Breton as a second language. With the zeal of the convert they established in September 1918 the political movement that came to be commonly known by the name of its newspaper, *Breiz Atao*. In 1927 it became an official political party and took part in the 1930 elections. *Breiz Atao*'s political ideology had developed its autonomist tendencies and it fought the election on the platform of self-rule for Brittany within the framework of France. It performed very badly in those elections and the following year decided to adopt the name *Parti National Breton* (*Strollad Broadel Breiz*), echoing the pre-war association.

The supporters of *Breiz Atao* were a very small minority within the population. It has been suggested that there were at the very most between 1,000 and 2,000 activists, although the circulation of *Breiz Atao* in 1934 regularly reached 5,000. One event that did increase support for the party, albeit temporarily, was the blowing up, in 1932, of the offending union of France and Brittany statue in Rennes. This was supposedly the work of the militant secret society *Gwenn-ha-Du*, and the French authorities' overreaction to all sorts of Breton associations, including quite respectable cultural ones as well as the political, provoked some sympathy for the cause and the PNB's membership increased somewhat.

In the 1936 elections the PNB changed tactics by supporting the candidates who agreed with its more moderate policies, such as the right to teach Breton in schools and regional devolution. Fifteen of the candidates were elected.

As well as being a political voice the paper *Breiz Atao* also sponsored a literary journal called *Gwalarn*. Originally a supplement to *Breiz Atao* the journal was published independently from 1925 onwards and did much to promote a modern Breton literature written in literary standard Breton. Under its visionary editor Roparz Hemon it fostered talented authors such as Jakez Riou and Youenn Drezen.

There were other more moderate political elements in the *Emsav* also such as the left-wing movement *War Zao*, and the pre-war cultural association *Bleun Brug*, which continued to be very active. Another moderate movement was ABES (*Ar Brezoneg er Skol* – Breton in schools) that aimed to achieve one thing, the teaching of Breton in schools. It succeeded in gaining the support of 207 communes in 1936 and 305 in 1938. As for the pre-war associations, the URB now existed more or less in name only, while the FRB struggled to overcome the differences between its Breton-speaking members from the west and the Gallo-speaking members from the east, most of whom had joined after the war.

Breton nationalists tended to be right wing in their ideology, and some were more extreme than others, but it was trade unionism that found favour with many people in the industrial areas. The socialists gradually took control of the municipal councils in Brest, Rennes and Lorient while Douarnenez even voted in a communist mayor in 1921, the first in France.

This growth in urban socialism was perceived as a threat by the leaders of the *Office Central des Associations Agricoles de Landerneau*. Founded in 1906, this peasant organisation's aim was to improve the lot of Breton farmers. Its membership increased after the war and it established branches throughout Finistère and the Morbihan. It arranged agricultural courses, campaigned for better leasehold terms for tenants, organized supplies of cheap fertilizer and set up an insurance fund for its members. But the Landerneau association, and others like it, was also about the political control of peasants. Led by squires and landowning gentry the association was eager for its members to remain faithful to the vision of a traditional rural society where landowner and peasant lived in social harmony. The leaders encouraged political conservatism among their members.

The FSPO (*Fédération des syndicats paysan de l'Ouest*) saw things differently. This agricultural syndicate, founded in Upper Brittany in the 1920s by a group of priests associated with the Catholic democratic newspaper *Ouest-Éclair*, was one of a group known as the *syndicats des cultivateurs-cultivants* (syndicates of labouring farmers).

While imitating the Landerneau association in offering practical help the FSPO argued for a new social rural order where the rich landlords could no longer exploit their tenants.

It should be noted that the Landernau-type syndicates were most successful in those areas where *chouannerie* had been rife in the previous century, that is to say in white areas, while the FSPO and its ilk found most support in the blue areas.

Alongside the agricultural syndicates and urban trade unions the Catholic associations of the JAC (*Jeunesse Agricole Chrétienne*) and JOC (*Jeunesse Ouvrière Chrétienne*) were also active among the youth. These associations sprung up in the 1930s to combat the secularisation of society and they were well supported in Brittany. The church was still very powerful in parts of rural Brittany and in fact the number of young men who chose to train for the priesthood after the war escalated, although large numbers of them went abroad to practise as official French policy continued to be negative towards the church. The local bishop could still influence daily life as did the authoritarian bishop Mgr Duparc of Finistère, who dominated his flock for twenty years and provoked anti-clerical reactions in the towns of communist Douarnenez and more moderate Quimper.

The activities of the agricultural syndicates and associations did ameliorate conditions for some Breton farmers but the general improvement in agriculture was still very gradual. The average size of a farm in the Côtes-du-Nord was still only 9.06 hectares in 1929 and this had only increased to 9.7 hectares by 1946. Despite this the amount of land worked by owner-farmers, as opposed to tenant-farmers, was 52 per cent in 1929, although the percentage decreased again during the Depression. Most of the farms continued to be self-sustaining in that they grew crops and kept animals mostly for their own consumption, and only sold what was surplus to requirement. Some specialization existed, such as the early vegetables on the mild northern coast, while the southern coast supported farms which specialized in peas and green beans for the canning industry. Life remained hard for most agricultural labourers, although the gradual introduction of machinery such as reapers and threshing machines helped the workload of male labourers. The lack of electricity on most farms meant that the women still did tasks such as churning by hand. Even in 1944 only a third of the rural population of Côtes-du-Nord had electricity.

Breton industry, in the aftermath of the First World War, contributed to the effort of rebuilding the country. The arsenals and naval works aided the reconstruction of the military and merchant navy while new industries that had appeared during the war, like the railway construction works at Nantes and the aeronautical industry at Saint-Nazaire and Bouguenais (*Kervegon*), continued to develop. As products such as fertilizers and chemicals developed, and new methods in food processing appeared, Brittany opened up new factories, producing for example biscuits, chocolate and soap.

However, as before, nearly all the industrial development was taking place in the Loire Basin, leaving the rest of the country with only scattered minor and under-invested enterprises. Even where there were flourishing commercial enterprises, industrial development was hampered by the fact that so many of the owners were outsiders. The breweries of Nantes, Rennes and Brest were controlled by an American firm, a Dutch–British company owned the soap factory at Nantes, and a New York firm had control of the maritime charters of nearly all the ports on the south coast of Brittany. These foreign companies inevitably put profit before any concern about developing Brittany.

Fishing continued to be important to the Breton economy and the inter-war period saw the appearance of new quays and jetties and a purpose-built fishing harbour was constructed at Lorient. Sardines were still a major catch on the south coast but Concarneau now became the main European port for tuna. In their now motorized boats the men of Camaret and Douarnenez fished for *langoustine* while cod remained the mainstay of Saint-Malo's fish industry.

Tourism continued to bloom; rail visitors were now increasingly joined by those who came by car. New scenic routes were built for the tourist driver and villas, chalets, hotels, casinos, pleasure harbours and golf courses mushroomed along the coast. The resort of La Baule in particular developed at a spectacular rate: the thirty hotels and 1,043 villas it possessed in 1921 had multiplied to 180 hotels and 2,400 villas by 1929.

The tourist industry, like every other economic activity, slowed down when the Depression hit Brittany in the 1930s. Agriculture was the first sector to suffer as food prices plunged, partly as a result of over-production. The costs of running a farm remained the same however and many peasants who had recently bought their own farms now fell into debt and had to sell them again. Labour costs, on the other hand, had actually risen as the law of 1928 meant that farmers had to pay national insurance contributions on behalf of their workers. It was the small farms that were the most vulnerable as they were poorly organized and defenceless against the powerful middle men.

Many rural areas reacted to the crisis by supporting the radical right-wing Henri Dorgères. His movement, the *Défense Paysanne* and its youth branch the *Chemises Vertes* (Green Shirts) was popular throughout west France; mass meetings were organized with thousands of peasants flocking to hear his speeches. Dorgères' political stance was similar to the Landerneau association's conservative anti-state intervention attitude but his Green Shirts were responsible for more violent actions. For example they tried to force the canneries of south Finistère to raise the price they paid farmers for their peas by vandalising the factory. They also disrupted the meetings of left-wing activists and acted against striking agricultural workers. The movement itself was short-lived and this rural fascism did not develop into anything more but it did reflect rural discontent and the feeling that the state did not care about the countryside.

In fact it would seem that the French state did not care too much about Breton economy at all as some major economic decisions that it took during the 1930s had devastating effects. For example, it ignored the adverse effect on the Breton canneries when it agreed to import 1,350,000 Spanish tins so that Spain would import French cars, even though the national French consumption of canned food was only 1,200,000 tins per annum, and Brittany produced 700,000 tins a year. In 1931 Paris imposed a quota on the import of British coal and it insisted that Brittany buy French coal. This was in order to protect the coal producers of north-eastern France, but the decision completely disregarded the effect this had on Brittany where, as well as having to buy more expensive but lower quality French coal, the economy suffered when the British retaliated by reducing their imports of early French vegetables, most of which came from Brittany.

The economic crisis hit industry as well as agriculture, especially in Nantes where the soapworks, biscuit factories and sugar refineries all laid off workers. The sweet factory of Cossé-Duval closed down altogether in 1934. Trade dropped off and Saint-Nazaire sank to sixteenth place in the port league of France. In 1933 the *département* of Loire-Inférieure had the dubious honour of being the sixth worse *département* in France for unemployment. Hunger marches and strikes ensued throughout Brittany, with the 1932 strike of the shoe workers at Fougères lasting eight months. In August 1935 barricades were built at Brest, street battles were fought, buildings were placed under siege and two workers were killed, when state salaries were cut.

Ironically it was the threat of war that pulled Brittany out of the economic doldrums. The arsenals and naval shipyards were essential components in the race to re-arm and the oil refinery at Donges (*Donez*), which had been built in 1932, now became vital along with the aeronautical works: both industries were nationalized. The canning industry benefited directly from the Spanish Civil War as its main competitor was now eliminated. Even tourism picked up again, although this was largely due to the introduction of the paid holiday in 1936. In that year Brittany received 550,000 visitors, many of whom were exiles returning home for a break.

But while the arms factories and naval ports were busily getting ready for the forthcoming conflict, there were others getting ready for the war with Germany in a different way. During the 1930s the more extreme elements of the PNB, under the leadership of Olier Mordrel and Fañch Debauvais, had developed an admiration for fascism and as their pronouncements became increasingly anti-French the two men had to escape over the border to Belgium in August 1939 to avoid arrest. The paper *Breiz Atao* was suppressed and the PNB was made illegal. Mordrel and Debauvais based themselves in Germany where they drew up plans on what role Brittany could play within the new Europe of German domination.

The number of Breton nationalists who agreed with Mordrel and Debauvais in seeing the forthcoming war with Germany as a golden opportunity for Brittany was literally a handful, and their actions and beliefs were completely out of step with the rest of the population who regarded Germany as the enemy.

10

The Second World War to the present day

Although the number of Bretons who died in the Second World War was lower than the figure for the First World War, it left much deeper physical scars on the countryside itself. Complete neighbourhoods were destroyed, the coast became one mass of concrete and barbed wire and the whole population suffered deprivation as it struggled with shortages of food and basic commodities. Added to this was the shock of being occupied by an enemy army.

After the defeat of the French army and the withdrawal of allied troops at Dunkirk the German invasion of Brittany was swift. The German troops marched on Rennes on 18 June 1940; they were in Brest on the 19th and had reached Lorient by 21 June. On 22 June Marshall Pétain signed the armistice treaty with Hitler at Compiègne and the period of German occupation began.

Brittany was in a strategically important position and so the German navy quickly built bases here to accommodate their submarines. Huge installations were constructed at Brest, Lorient and Saint-Nazaire in a matter of months. This was the main reason why Brittany suffered so much from Allied bombings. The three naval towns were targeted along with Nantes and Saint-Malo and most of their inhabitants were evacuated to the countryside. Nantes was bombed twenty-eight times and 1,000 bombs were dropped here on one night alone in September 1943. Even towns that were less important from a military point of view such as Morlaix and Rennes were targeted. By the liberation in June 1944 Brest, Lorient and Saint-Nazaire had been practically razed to the ground. In Brest 90 per cent of all the buildings were either completely demolished or damaged and in Saint-Nazaire only 100 houses were left intact in 1945 out of a total of 8,000. Saint-Malo was almost totally destroyed as well but here some of the damage was inflicted during the street battles at the end of the occupation in August 1944.

Brittany's geographical position made the German Reich fear that its coast could be used for landing enemy troops allowing the allies to develop a second front. So Brittany was included when work began in 1942 on the construction of the Atlantic Wall along the north-west seaboard of Europe. This entailed peppering the coastline with concrete blockhouses, barbed wire, minefields and anti-tank traps. Houses were demolished to make way for firing ranges and the coastal communities had their able-bodied men and carts requisitioned to contribute to the construction work.

One of the major preoccupations of the country at this time was how to provide enough food to feed everybody. Agricultural products were scarce due to the shortage of labour, chemical fertilizer, fodder and fuel, and the situation was only made worse by inclement weather which caused poor crop yields. Yet rural Brittany was expected to contribute supplies of food to the cities along with feeding the extra mouths of prisoners of war, refugees and the occupying army. Despite the deprivation countless families strived to send as many food parcels as possible to the 137,000 Breton prisoners of war in Germany.

Breton fishermen also had it hard during the occupation. They suffered from lack of fuel and ice and found themselves under threat from both German and British attacks. In 1941, for example, Douarnenez lost about sixty of its fishermen at sea, victims of submarine and aerial attacks.

There were a few, a very small number, who welcomed the opportunities that the German occupation seemed to offer them. The leaders of the banned PNB, Mordrel and Debauvais, were both condemned to death as traitors in May 1940. But with the occupation of Brittany the following month they returned from their exile in Germany believing that the time had come for Brittany to play her part within the framework of the new Europe under Hitler. The PNB leaders gathered together some members to form the *Comité National Breton* (*Kuzul Broadel Breiz*) and they drew up a constitution for the new Breton state that they hoped was on the horizon. They launched a weekly newspaper, *l'Heure Bretonne*, in July and initially this had a readership of over 30,000. This figure dropped as other newspapers appeared and so provided an alternative source of news for the information hungry population. *L'Heure Bretonne*'s readership also fell away as it became clear that the Germans were not going to release the Breton prisoners of war despite their initial promise to the PNB. The numbers of people who were actually members of the PNB is estimated at about 2,500–3,000 at its climax in 1942–3. This represented about 0.1 per cent of the population.

France had its collaborationist political parties as well such as the RNP (*Rassemblement National Populaire*) and the PPF (*Parti Populaire Française*) and these also had members in Brittany. It is estimated that between 0.1 and 0.2 per cent of the population were active in the collaborationist parties in Brittany, mostly in Ille-et-Vilaine. There were others who also tried to turn the situation to their advantage; for example it is estimated that about 1 per cent of the population of Rennes collaborated with the occupiers, either directly or indirectly.

It was common for the collaborationist parties to have a military wing; about 6,000 Frenchmen are believed to have worn the German uniform and fought for Germany either in the LVF (*Légion de Volontaires Française contre le Bolchévisme*) or the *Waffen SS*. The PNB's official military wing was the *Bagad Stourm* and about 500 young people went through its ranks. Despite the uniform, which included an armband adorned with a *triskell* and high boots, their activities seem to have been restricted mostly to exercises in the woods and singing patriotic songs.

More infamous was the paramilitary group *Bezen Perrot*. Originally called *Lu Brezhon* it changed its name in 1944 in honour of father Perrot, a patriotic and highly respected priest who had been murdered by the *Résistance*. The founder and leader of the group, Neven Henaff (Célestin Lainé), was an admirer of the IRA and a pro-Nazi. He offered the services of his unit to the Germans and they became members of the SD

(*Sicherheitsdienst der SS*). They fought alongside the German police in campaigns against the *Résistance*, burned down farmhouses, took prisoners and engaged in pitched battles with members of the maquis also. Their infamy far outshined their actual contribution to collaboration and it is estimated that their members between December 1943 and May 1945 numbered no more than seventy-two. Yet news of their activities spread throughout Brittany and they were often confused with *Bagad Stourm*. Their actions did much to foster the belief that all members of the *Emsav* were collaborators and traitors.

Most Bretons however viewed the Germans with suspicion and followed a 'wait and see' policy, they did not actively collaborate but they did not actively resist either. Their attitude towards Marshall Pétain was in tune with most of the French population as a whole. They regarded him as their saviour. Many agreed with the view that the blame for the sudden and easy conquest lay with the weaknesses of the politics of the Third Republic and they looked forward to building a new France. Others simply saw him as a hero who could offer some stability at a difficult time. When he was voted full powers on 10 July 1940 in Vichy only a handful of Breton deputies opposed him. Although Brittany was in the occupied zone and was thus directly under the authority of the Germans the Vichy regime was still responsible for the civil jurisdiction here.

There were aspects of the ideology of the Vichy regime which were attractive to many conservative Bretons. The talk of returning to traditional and Catholic values and the importance given to families and small businesses was music to the ears of many conservatives. The regime's policy of decentralisation and provincialism struck a chord with those who still harboured a reactionary nostalgia for pre-Revolutionary days. The promotion of the corporatist system was welcomed by that sector of the rural world that had been influenced by Dorgerist propaganda the previous decade.

Those Bretons who cared for the language and identity of the land, but who did not seek independence, welcomed Vichy's apparent regionalism. Their wish was an acknowledgment of

Brittany as a unique region within France. One such person was Yann Fouéré and he was responsible for the newspaper *La Bretagne*. This daily newspaper published news from a Breton point of view and its aim was to foster regionalism and offer an alternative to the autonomist policies of the PNB.

Fouére was also the second general secretary of the *Comité Consultatif de Bretagne*. This body, made up of respectable and prominent members of Breton society of all political shades (except the PNB) was appointed by the French regional prefect and was thus the first institution to represent Brittany to the French government since 1789. It had no powers as such; rather its role was purely consultative. Its main concern was the promotion and protection of Brittany's heritage in the form of patrimony, folklore and language and it attempted to minimize the damage to local monuments by the German forces. For example, the *Comité* intervened in order to save an ancient chapel and some bronze statues of famous Bretons from destruction. Towards the end of the occupation it was also campaigning for the release of the prisoners of war and for more consideration to be given to the Breton economy. In 1944 it had the support of more than 200 local councils and 1,000 prominent Bretons had voiced their support. Most of the members were pro-Vichy but there were pro-Gaullists among them and some were even active in the *Résistance*. Many members at the end of the war were genuinely surprised to be regarded as traitors because of their involvement with the *Comité*.

The Vichy government did very little for Brittany however. Communes with more than 2,000 population lost the right to elect their own mayor and when France was divided into administrative regions in June 1941 Brittany found that the Loire-Inférieure had been attached to the neighbouring region. Despite Vichy's fondness for history and tradition the Breton pleas to have the Loire-Inférieure included once more fell on deaf ears. This amputation of the Loire-Inférieure left Brittany as an almost exclusively agricultural region and despite post-war governments' claims of the illegality of the Vichy administration this is one issue that has still not been rectified.

As the war progressed however the people gradually began to turn against the Vichy government. After the defeat at Stalingrad in 1943 Germany no longer looked invincible and as hostages were taken and shot in revenge for *Résistance* actions they felt more and more uneasy. There is evidence of a negative attitude to Vichy in Brittany as early as the middle of 1941 when ministers on a visit were treated very coldly. Reports showed that public opinion was changing and from 1942 more and more mayors and councillors were resigning their posts.

The real turning point came in February 1943 with the implementation of the STO (*Service du Travail Obligatoire*). This measure was a way of solving the acute shortage of labour that Germany was experiencing by forcing French people to go and work there. Initially agricultural workers, students and women were exempt but gradually, with Germany desperate for more workers each month, they were included also. Many decided to go into hiding or join the maquis rather than be part of Germany's war machine.

Even before the STO was introduced industrial workers in Brittany had suffered. On 23 October 1942, 688 specialists from the arms factory in Brest were forced to go and work in Hamburg. Factories in Nantes were closed down as the workers left for Germany and in some factories in Saint-Nazaire and Trignac (*Trigneg*) the machines themselves were transported to Germany.

Thus from 1943 onwards the activities of the *Résistance* increased although a small number of people had decided from the very outset that they would do their utmost to oppose the Germans. The most famous case was Ile-de-Sein (*Enez-Sun*). In June 1940 the whole able-bodied male population of this small island, all 130 of them, sailed across to Britain to join De Gaulle and the future Free French Forces.

The *Résistance* became much more active after 1943 and its members took part in actions such as derailing trains, sabotaging electric pylons and blowing up lorries. Occasionally German personnel were targeted and it was in retaliation for the attack on lieutenant colonel Hotz that twenty-seven hostages were shot at Châteaubriant. The *Résistance* also published clandestine newspapers and listened to the secret broadcasts from London. They provided information to the allies and helped shot-down pilots escape. They were also responsible for executing perceived collaborators and from 1943 until the end of the war thirty-three members of the *Emsav* were killed by them. The Breton resistant fighters were very young and they included very few peasants. The actual numbers of active resistants were very small, about 1–2 per cent, which was similar to the rest of France. As the defeat of Germany appeared increasingly inevitable the numbers swelled, especially in 1944. Yet there were regional differences and it is noticeable that people in the traditionally white Brittany joined much later than the blue areas.

For four years Brittany was under German occupation and Vichy administration yet some individuals saw this as no reason for them to renounce their personal efforts to preserve and develop the Breton language and culture. In fact, to a certain extent, there were important cultural developments during this period. For the first time official permission was granted for Breton (and the other regional languages) to be taught in school and the first ever Breton-medium school was founded in 1942 as a private initiative. It was partly because of this development in education that the Breton orthography was unified; but although it is widely used today some still regard this orthography (called *peurunvan*) as being a German-inspired deviation and they refuse to use it. Other breakthroughs included the broadcasting of Breton on the radio for the first time and the establishment of a Breton-language weekly newspaper (*Arvor*). A Celtic Institute was set up to promote Breton language and culture. The conference papers of this body reveal idealistic and ambitious plans for a future Brittany whose culture would be nurtured in the New Europe. Although all of these developments were cultural activities they have sometimes been criticized by later genera-tions as an example of Breton collaborationism. In 1998 the name of a Breton-medium high school was changed because it had been named after Roparz Hemon, one of the most active and respected people in the language movement from 1925–75, but who had been prominent in fostering cultural developments during the war.

The beginning of the end of the occupation came with the allied landings in June 1944. Most of Brittany was liberated after bloody battles that summer but the naval strongholds of Lorient and Saint-Nazaire held out until May 1945. With the Liberation came the purges and many activists of the Breton movement were arrested as collaborators. Some of the worst offenders such as Mordrel and Lainé escaped abroad and the small number who were found guilty and executed were mostly members of *Bezen Perrot.* The vast majority were released after the initial chaotic period although some such as Roparz Hemon were forbidden to live in Brittany for several years afterwards.

Brittany's post-war history was one of recovery and renewal as it rebuilt its bombed cities, modernized its agriculture and developed new industries. Farming in particular developed in leaps and bounds and the farms of the end of the twentieth century were a world apart from those of 1945.

The first step was electrification and mechanization but in the immediate post-war period the number of farms remained the same. Rural exodus continued as agriculture became less labour intensive. The nature of the countryside changed as hedges and banks were ripped down and flattened as the typical *bocage* scenery made way for the larger fields and machinery. Through the course of the half-century the number of farms decreased and they grew steadily bigger. In the 1950s two-thirds of Breton farms were less than ten hectares; by 1988 the average was nineteen hectares and by 2000 the average Breton farm was thirty-three hectares. The number of farms at the turn of the millennium was 51,200, half the number in 1988.

New techniques were developed as agriculture intensified and Brittany became the leading producer in France for pigs, poultry, eggs and milk. In 2005 it had more dairy cows than any other French region. Its early vegetables, already important before the war, became even more productive as improvements in the transport system enabled more efficient distribution of goods. The main vegetable products throughout the post-war period and up to the present day were fresh cauliflower, artichokes, potatoes, and tomatoes while peas and French beans were mostly grown for preserving.

The success of Breton agriculture in using innovative methods was partly the result of change in the peasant mentality. A new generation of activists had taken over the leadership of the old farmers' movements and cooperatives and they forced farmers to accept new methods and ideas. They were also active in promoting farmers' rights and in voicing their grievances. The most famous of these new generation leaders was Alexis Gourvennec. He was one of the leaders of the May 1961 protest which flared up when the farmers saw their prices drop once more as a result of a glut of potatoes and vegetables. What began as a local protest about the archaic marketing system spread throughout western France and it became one of the biggest and most effective peasant demonstrations in post-war France.

Gourvennec had also been responsible, the previous year, for organizing a convoy of lorries to transport artichokes directly to Paris where the farmers sold their vegetables directly on the streets as a protest against avaricious middlemen. But Gourvennec is better known for being the founder of the only farmers' cooperative ferry company in Europe, Brittany Ferries. In the mid-1960s he and his pressure group from north Finistère succeeded in persuading the government to invest in the building of a deep-water port in western Brittany. Gourvennec had his eye on Britain as a potential market for the early vegetables and he wanted to see a direct transport link there in time for Britain's probable entry into the EEC (European Economic Community). However after the port was built at Roscoff no ferry company was willing to use the new facilities. In answer to this problem Gourvennec's agricultural cooperative launched their own ferry service in 1973 and it transported vegetables, heavy freight and tourists to Plymouth. The highly successful company later opened a second line from Saint-Malo to Portsmouth and it went on to offer services to Ireland and Spain also. While today the main cargo is tourists and their vehicles Gourvennec's farmers still owned 64 per cent of Brittany Ferries' shares in 1999.

France had entered the EEC in 1957 and Brussels' agricultural policies did not always benefit Breton farmers, especially as those policies were often made with the interest of cereal farmers in mind: cereal farming was relatively uncommon in Brittany. One policy that hit Brittany particularly hard was the imposition of milk quotas. Many farmers who had invested heavily in new machinery and installations in the expectation of increasing profits now found themselves in debt.

Perhaps one of the most important problems facing Breton farmers at the threshold of the twenty-first century is pollution. The new farming methods, especially the intensified use of chemical fertilizers and pesticides, are partly to blame for the increased pollution in Brittany. One difficulty for pig-breeders in particular is that nitrate from liquid manure has contaminated underground rivers and streams, endangering water supplies. Nor are the modern farms spared the vagaries of the weather: the droughts of 1976, 1988–92 and 2006 affected the farms here as elsewhere. Nevertheless Brittany remains one of the main active agricultural regions of France and is responsible for 13 per cent of the sales turnover of French agricultural production.

Fishing is another traditional activity that has had to adapt to new techniques and seek out new markets. The number of boats steadily decreased during the post-war period and they became motorized and increased in size. The larger vessels installed freezing facilities on board. Initially the catches almost doubled between 1947 and 1958 and the modernizing of the fishing fleet in the years 1955–60 increased the amounts even further; but as fishing stocks depleted and competition became more fierce the Breton fishing industry began to suffer. The 1970s saw Scandinavian and Icelandic cod competing directly with Saint-Malo's fishermen and the 200-mile fishing zone imposed in 1977 was the final straw for many as they now had to travel further and further afield to seek their fish. While the traditional tuna and sardine fishing ports of Concarneau, Douarnenez and Guilvenec have remained important, the second most important fishing port in France today is Lorient. As well as increasing its tonnage of fish from 32,000 in the 1960s to almost 50,000 tonnes in 1990 the port is a base for several freezing factories and canneries. It also houses various research centres and colleges that are all devoted to studying fishing methods and products. Indeed Lorient's fish in 1992 provided more employment for bureaucrats, researchers and teachers than it did fishermen.

The fishing crisis of the 1970s was exacerbated by the oil crisis that caused the price of fuel to rise fourfold. Other contributory factors were overfishing and the dumping of cheap white fish on the market by Russia. The fishermen had no one with the charisma and organisation of Gourvennec to lead them but they did take their cue from the agricultural protests when in 1993–4 conditions had got so bad for some of them that they decided to riot. It was during one of their demonstrations that the historic *Parlement* building at Rennes was burned down.

A new development appeared in the Breton fishing industry in the 1960s with the establishment of oyster and mussel commercial beds. The main area for shellfish farming today is near Brest and Plouguerneau while the bay of Morlaix has also been successful with breeding salmon. In 1990 the company Salmor harvested 1,200 tonnes there. In 2005 there were 700 businesses involved in fish and shellfish farming, employing about 2,300. Unfortunately the shellfish beds are also in danger from water pollution from chemicals and oil spillages.

In 2005 80 per cent of the Breton fleet consisted of offshore or inshore boats, reflecting the decline in deep-sea fishing. The number of fishermen had decreased to 6,000, compared with the 20,000 that were active before the war. Nevertheless Breton boats are still responsible for 40 per cent of the fish caught off France and the whole annual production for fish and crustaceans in 2002 was 162,000 tonnes.

Brittany's industrial infrastructure also changed dramatically during the post-war period. Most of the small family firms involved in the traditional industries of shoe and paper making and vegetable and fish canning disappeared. The occasional Breton enterprise managed to survive despite competition, for example businesses such as the biscuit company of Traou Mad in Pont-Aven and Hénaff that produced 40 million tins of pâté in

1988. Industrial developments saw more companies relocating here as France followed a policy of encouraging industry to move away from overcrowded Paris. The most obvious example of this is the car maker Citroën who opened a factory in Rennes in 1951 and another one in 1961, providing employment for 10,000. The availability of cheap labour also attracted companies and factories in the field of electronics, textiles, chemicals and metallurgy. Ship building continued to be important with the docks at Brest and Lorient supplying the French navy, while the main centres for civil shipbuilding were Concarneau, Brest, Saint-Malo and Lorient. However today 43 per cent of the industrial companies in Brittany (not including the *département* of Loire-Atlantique) are involved in some way with the food industry, reflecting the developments in Brittany's agriculture.

Tourism continued to grow during the latter part of the twentieth century as standards of living rose and Brittany became much more accessible. New motorways and dual carriage ways were built and the fast TGV train service extended to Rennes, Brest and Quimper. The direct ferry routes and cheap air fares to regional airports made the country more accessible than ever to foreigners and related industries such as crêpe making and local ceramics also flourished. It was partly with tourism in mind that the *département* Côtes-du-Nord changed its name in 1990 to the more romantic sounding Côtes-d'Armor. Nevertheless the industry sometimes suffered temporary setbacks caused by pollution, such as the 15 per cent drop in visitors in 2000 following the oil spill from the tanker *Erika*.

Brittany is no longer the backward region it once was and some of the immediate post-war economic success can be attributed to CELIB. CELIB (*Comité d'Etudes et de Liaison des Intérêts Breton*), founded in 1949, was a federation of representatives from all sectors of the Breton economy. This organization, which became a parliamentary commission in 1951, lobbied the French government with its reports and proposals. It did much to ensure that Brittany was included in the French economic development plans of 1954–8 although the government still considered the region as being only four *départements*. The fifth *département*, Loire-Inférieure, had its name changed to Loire-Atlantique in 1957 and was considered to be part of the artificial region of Pays de Loire.

CELIB's regionalism was economic and this was deemed acceptable in the years immediately after the war; but manifestation of any kind of political nationalism was impossible during this period. The memory of the PNB's wartime activities was too fresh. Most of the prominent leaders of the Breton movement were either in prison or exiled and it was left to the younger generation to rekindle the flame. Initially they concentrated on cultural activities only and various Celtic Circles were founded where people learned and practised traditional folk music and dances, as a new generation of Bretons rediscovered their roots. The organization BAS (*Bodadeg ar Sonerien*) was founded in 1946 to promote Breton bagpipe bands and by 1950 it had 1,000 members. It is still very active today. The 1970s saw the beginning of the revival of the *fest-noz*, communal traditional dances, and Breton music was made popular by the likes of Alan Stivell who did much to resurrect the Celtic harp. Breton traditional music and dance remain very popular today.

Some of the pre-war cultural developments reappeared discreetly as *Bleun Brug* and *Ar Falz* resumed their activities. The cultural review *Al Liamm* was launched in 1946 and to a very large extent it was a continuation of *Gwalarn* under a new editor, Ronan Huon. (Roparz Hemon was living in exile in Ireland and he died there in 1975.)

As time passed Breton political feelings were allowed expression once more. The socialist green UDB (*Union Démocratique Bretonne*) was founded in 1964 and the more right wing SAV (*Strollad ar Vro*) appeared in 1973. They both fielded candidates in elections but without much success. *Emgann*, which seeks complete independence for Brittany, was established in 1983. The latest political party to be established is *Parti Breton* (*Holl a unan* in Breton) in 2001, which looks to the nationalist Welsh party of *Plaid Cymru* and the SNP (Scottish Nationalist Party) for inspiration.

Other more extremist elements also emerged, the most infamous being the FLB (*Front de Libération de la Bretagne*), founded in 1965, who were responsible for damaging the television mast of Roc-Tredudon in 1974 and blowing up the Hall of Mirrors in the palace of Versailles in 1978. They saw themselves as the heirs of the pre-war *Gwenn-ha-Du* secret organization; they continued their attacks on property until 1981. Another similar organization was the ARB (*Armée Révolutionnaire de Bretagne*). In 2000 Breton extremists were accused of blowing up a McDonald's restaurant near Dinan when one person was killed.

Extremist actions aside, the Breton movement today finds itself regarded much more favourably by the general population than ever before and the attitudes toward the Breton language have experienced a complete about-turn. A poll commissioned by the newspaper *Le Télégramme* and the TV channel *France 3* in 1997 reported that 88 per cent of the population wanted to see the language survive and 80 per cent were in favour of Breton being taught in schools. In 2001 a similar poll demonstrated that 92 per cent of Bretons regarded the language in a positive light. While the numbers of speakers (estimated at 300,000 in 2005) may still be falling the number of people learning the language afresh is growing (8,000 in 2005), as is the number of Breton medium schools run by *Diwan*. The first *Diwan* school was opened in 1977 and this was followed by the introduction of bilingual streams in state schools in 1984 (*Div-yezh*) and in Catholic schools (*Dihun*) in 1990. In 2005 the number of children who were receiving all or some of their education through the medium of Breton in the five *départements* was 9,700.

The proliferation of local radio stations in more recent years has provided new platforms for the dissemination of Breton but the cable channel *TV Breizh*, established in 2000, has so far failed to increase substantially the number of hours that Breton is broadcast annually on television.

While the majority of Bretons appear to be supportive of the Breton language, there has also been a change of attitude towards Gallo. The Gallo movement was inspired by the example of the

Emsav and Gallo folklore began to be collected seriously in the 1950s by Simone Morand and Albert Poulain. The associations *Maézoe* and *Bertaèyn Galeizz*, both founded in 1978, aim to promote the language and every year the *Assembiés Gallèses*, a week of activities to celebrate Gallo, is held in various places in Upper Brittany.

Although Brittany might seem to be revelling today in its historical and regional identity there is one aspect of life, which at one time was regarded by some as being crucial to Breton identity, which has seen a dramatic decline. The Catholic church here, like elsewhere in France, has been decisively rejected as the number of churchgoers has plummeted since the 1950s. The church in Brittany no longer sees the Breton language as its ally, and apart from the actions of some remarkable individual priests, the link between the faith and the Breton language no longer exists.

Brittany's demographical make-up also changed during the post-war period. The traditional rural exodus continued initially as agriculture became less labour intensive and while many went to seek new opportunities in the towns of Brest, Rennes and Nantes and along the coast, most of the young people leaving headed for Paris. This emigration meant that Brittany's population in the 1950s and 1960s was an ageing one, and even when the number of people moving in to the region increased this only exacerbated the problem as most of the immigrants were elderly Bretons returning to their homeland to retire. Some regions in the interior were particularly hard hit by emigration; for example the population of Carhaix fell by 25 per cent between 1954 and 1962. Yet from 1975 onwards emigration began to slow down as more job opportunities were developed and gradually the trend of an ageing population was reversed. In 2005 24.1 per cent of Bretons (of the four *départements*) were under 21 in a population of 2,979,000 (excluding the Loire-Altantique).

Thus Brittany enters the twenty-first century as an economically developed country with a population that is young, vibrant and confident. Although officially consisting of only four *départements*, Brittany to most people, be they historians, visitors or Bretons themselves, still includes the Loire-Atlantique. The ducal castle in Nantes is visible proof of this region's important contribution to Breton history, and the passionate campaign to re-include the city and its surrounding area is evidence of the strong feeling of identity and pride in the past that Bretons feel today despite the vast linguistic, cultural and economic influences of France.

Bibliography

Ardagh, J., *The New France: A Society in Transition 1945–1977* (Harmondsworth, 1977)

—— *France in the New Century: Portrait of a Changing Society* (London, 1999)

Astill, G. and Davies, W., *A Breton Landscape* (London, 1997)

Baumgartner, F. J., *France in the Sixteenth Century* (London, 1995)

Bender, B., *The Archaeology of Brittany, Normandy and the Channel Islands: An Introduction and Guide* (London, 1986)

Bergin, J., *Cardinal Richelieu: Power and the Pursuit of Wealth* (New Haven, 1985)

Bowen, E. G., *Saints, Seaways and Settlements* (Cardiff, 1977)

Brékilien, Y., *La vie quotidienne des paysans bretons au XIXe siècle* (Paris, 1966)

Chadwick, N. K., *Early Brittany* (Cardiff, 1969)

Chédeville, A. and Tonnerre, N.-Y., *La Bretagne féodale XIe – XIIIe siècles* (Rennes, 1987)

Cunliffe, B., *Facing the Ocean: The Atlantic and its Peoples* (Oxford, 2001)

Davies, W., *Small Worlds: The Village Community in Early Medieval Brittany* (Duckworth, 1988)

Déniel, A., *Le Mouvement Breton 1919–1945* (Paris, 1976)

Dunbabin, J., *France in the Making 843–1180* (Oxford, 1985)

Élégoët, L., *Istor Breizh* (Sant Brieg, 1998)

Favereau, F., *Bretagne Contemporaine: Langue, Culture, Identité* (Morlaix, 1993)

Fleuriot, L., 'Yr ymfudo o Brydain i Lydaw', in G. Bowen (ed.), *Y Gwareiddiad Celtaidd*, (Llandysul, 1987)

Forrest, A., *Paris, the Provinces and the French Revolution* (London, 2004)

Galliou, P. and Jones, M., *The Bretons* (Oxford, 1991)

Gemie, S., *Brittany 1750–1950: The Invisible Nation*, (Cardiff: University of Wales Press, 2007)

Hallam, E., *Capetian France 987–1328*, (London/New York, 1980)

Hincks, R., *I Gadw Mamiaith Mor Hen* (Llandysul, 1995)

—— 'Ar vuoc'h koad', in *Llafar Gwlad*, 64 (May 1999)

Hutt, M., *Chouannerie and Counter-Revolution: Puisaye, the Princes and the British Government in the 1790s* (Cambridge, 1983)

Jones, M., *The Creation of Brittany: A Late Medieval State* (London, 1988)

—— *Ducal Brittany 1364–1399: Relations with England and France During the Reign of Duke John IV* (Oxford, 1970)

Knecht, R. J., *Richelieu: Profiles in Power* (Harlow, 1991)

Lagrée, M., *Religion et cultures en Bretagne 1850–1950* (Paris, 1992)

La Villemarqué, H. de, *Barzaz Breiz: Chants Populaires de la Bretagne* (Paris, 1939)

Le Duc, G., 'The colonisation of Brittany from Britain: New Approaches and Questions', in *Celtic Connections: Proceedings of 10th International Congress of Celtic Studies,* (East Linton, 1999)

Le Mat, J.-P., *Histoire de Bretagne* (Fouesnant, 2006)

Leguay, J.-P., and Martin, H., *Fastes et malheurs de la Bretagne ducal 1213–1532* (Rennes, 1982)

Mordrel, O., *Breiz Atao ou Histoire et Actualité du Nationalisme Breton* (Paris, 1973)

Minois, G., *Nouvelle Histoire de la Bretagne* (Paris, 1992)

Nicolas, M., *Histoire du Mouvement Breton* (Paris, 1982)

—— *Le Séparatisme en Bretagne* (Brasparts, 1986)

Piette, G. N., 'Tradition versus progress: the problem of modernising a minority: the case of Breton language and literature and the contribution of *Gwalarn*', in L. Touaf and S. Boutkhil (eds), *Minority Matters: Society, Theory, Literature: Proceedings of the 1st International Symposium on Minorities and Minor Literatures January 2004* (Oujda, 2005)

—— 'Saun le galo, poent de Bertaèyn: yr iaith Galo yn Llydaw', in *Breizh/Llydaw*, 41 (August 2005)

Raoul, L., *Geriadur ar Skrivagnerien ha yezhourien* (Montroulez, 1992)

Reece, J. E., *The Bretons against France: Ethnic Minority*

Nationalism in Twentieth Century Brittany (Chapel Hill, 1977)

Skol Vreizh, *Histoire de la Bretagne et des Pays Celtiques de 1789 à 1914. Tome 4.* (Morlaix, 1980)

—— *Histoire de la Bretagne et des Pays Celtiques. Des mégalithes aux cathédrales. Tome 1.* (Morlaix, 1983)

—— *Histoire de la Bretagne et des Pays Celtiques de 1914 à Nos Jours. Tome 5* (Morlaix, 1983)

—— *Histoire de la Bretagne et des Pays Celtiques. Tome 3. La Bretagne Province (1532–1789)* (Morlaix, 1986)

—— *Histoire de la Bretagne et des Pays Celtiques. Tome 2. L'État Breton (1341–1532)* (Morlaix, 1987)

Smith, J. M. H., *Province and Empire: Brittany and the Carolignians* (Cambridge, 1992)

Sutherland, D. M. G, *The Chouans: The Social Origins of Popular Counter-Revolution in Upper Brittany, 1770–1796* (Oxford, 1982)

—— *France 1789–1815: Revolution and Counterrevolution* (London, 1985)

Tanguy, B. and Lagrée, M., *Atlas d'Histoire de Bretagne* (Morlaix, 2002)

Tonnerre, N.-Y., 'Celtic literary tradition and the development of a feudal principality in Brittany', in H. Pryce (ed.), *Literacy in Medieval Celtic Societies* (Cambridge, 1998)

Treasure, G. R. R., *Seventeenth Century France* (London, 1966)

Pamphlet

Regional Council of Brittany, *Brittany Identity Card* (May 2005)

Websites

Dihun Breiz, *www.dihun.com*

Diwan, *www.diwanbreizh.org*

Mercator Media, *www.aber.ac.uk/~merwww/*
Ofis ar Brezhoneg, *www.ofis-bzh.org/*

Index

Act of Union 62
Agricola 21
agricultural techniques 103
agriculture
  change in peasant
      mentality 131
  developments 56
  improvement in 118
  pollution, and 132
  post–war
      developments 130–2
Aiguillon, duke of 80–2
Alan II 34–5
  Breton barons, and 37
Alan III
  marriage of 38
Alan IV 37–8
Alan the Great
  Vikings, and 33
Anne de Beaujeu 59
Anne of Brittany 60–1
  marriage of 60–1
Aquilonia Civitas 21
ARB 136
Ar Brezoneg er Skol 116–7
Ar Falz 135
archeological societies 111
Armorica 3–18
Arthur II 45
Arthur III 53
Arthur of Brittany 42
Assizes of Geoffrey 41
Atlantic seaway 14–15

Ballon, battle of 27
BAS 135
Berengar 34
Bertrand de Guesclin 52
Bezen Perrot 125–6
Bleun Brug 135
Bonnedou ru 73
Boursault
  release of prisoners 98
Breiz Atao 116
Brest
  economic success 75–6
Breton army
  Franco–Prussian war,
      and 111
Breton Association 88
Breton cavalry 25
Breton church
  absorption into French
      church 48
Breton economy 1380–1470
  56
Breton Kingdom,
  establishment of 19–35
Breton language 1–2
  abandonment by upper
      classes 36
  attitudes to 136
  ban on use 105–6
  church, and 106–7
  decline 35
Breton nobility
  exile 88
Brieg 21

Britain
    trade with 14–15
Britannia 19
Brittany
    geographical division 1
Brittany Ferries 131
British immigrations 19–35
    bishops 23
    churches 23
    Gallo–Romans, and 21
    Maximus, and 22
    numbers 20
    place–name studies 20
    plous 23
    political identity 23–4
    reasons for 22
    renunciation of Roman way
        of life 23
    Romans, consent of 22
    'saints' 23
    south–east Brittany 21
    third century 20
    upper Brittany 24
    Vannetais region 21–2
Bro Erec'h 23
Bronze Age 3–4
Buhez ar Sent 31

Carnac
    stone avenues 3
Carolingian miniscule
    script 32
Carrier, Jean–Baptiste
    death of priests, and 96
Catholic church
    decline of 137
Catholic League 65–6
CELIB 134
Celtic people 4–5
Celtic societies 111
Chamber of accounts 54
Chancellor 53
Charles VIII 59–60, 61
Charles de Bois 49–51
Charles de Valois 58–9

Charles the Bald 26–7
    defeat of 28
    Salomon, and 29–30
Chauvin, Guillaume 58
Chemises Vertes 120
Chouans
    Napoleon, and 100
    rebellion 97–9
church
    education, and 107–8
church buildings 109
civil war 65–74
    nature of 65
    Spanish troops 66
    strengthening of bond
        between Brittany and
        France 67–8
Civitates 11
Claude, duchess 61–2
Clovis 24
Colbert
    rebellion of 1675, and 72–3
Comité Consultatif de
    Bretagne 127
Conan II 38–9, 40
Condate 7, 11
Conlie 111–2
Conscription 93
Constance, duchess 41
    kidnapping of 41
Coriosolitae 5–6
Cornovia 23
coronation ritual 55
Crassius, Publius 8

d'Aumont, Marshal 67
Dagobert I 24–5
Darioritum 5
de La Borderie, Arthur
    Breton culture, and 110
de la Rouerie, Armand
    Tuffin 88
de Montesquiou, Marshal
    Dinan estates, and 79
de Pontcallec, marquis 79–80
Défense Paysanne 120

Demographical make–up
  change during post–war
    period 137
Départements
  creation of 88–9
depression
  effect of 119–20, 121
Dinan estates
  don gratuit, and 79
Diocletian 10
Diwan
  schools 136
Domain congéable 89
Dorgères, Henri 120
Duchy (936–1341) 36–48
  administrative system 45–6
  French Kings, and 45
  monasteries, and 47
  oscillation of position 37
  progression from
    overlord 36
  rules of neighbouring
    territories, and 38
  Saint–Malo 46
  urban growth 46–7
Dumnonia 23

ecclesiastical reform 36
economic decline 75–86
  climate, and 78
  diseases, and 78
  increased taxation 78–9
  intendant, and 78
  intermediary commission 80
education
  church, and 107–8
Edward III 50, 51
emigration 102–3
  Nantes, to 103–4
Emsav 11
enlightenment 84
Erispoé 28–29
estates 54
  role of 68–9
Estates General 83
  cahiers de doléances 85

Estates General 83 – contd
  elections 85
  format 83, 84
  sénéchaussée 85
Eudon de Porhöet 39

feudal society
  development of 37
fishing
  development 119
  post–war
    developments 132–3
fishing industry 104–5
  canning 104
FLB 136
fords 13
Fouéré, Yann 127
France and Brittany
  union 60–2
François I 53
François II 57
Franks
  border raids 24
  border with Bretons 24
  cultural influences 31–2
  empire 24
FRB 112
French Revolution 87–101
  aftermath 2
  centralization, and 88
  cheap bread, supply of 92–3
  Church, and 90–2
  conscription, and 93
  federalism, and 95–6
  guerrilla tactics of
    chouans 97
  onset of 75–86
  peasant uprising 1793 93–4
  priests, and 90–2, 98
  rural peasants, and 90
  urban bourgeoisie,
    and 89–90
  urban common people,
    and 92–3

French state
  economic decisions during
    1930s 120
Fronde insurgency 71–2
FSPO 117
Fulk the Red 33
Fundus 12
Fundus Victorianus 12

Gallo language 2
  attitudes to 136–7
Garum sauce 15
Gaulish language
  survival of 16
General assemblies 73
General council 53
Geoffrey I 40–1
  marriage of 38
Geoffrey of Monmouth 36
Golden Age 635
  cloth industry 63–74
  development of economy 63
  growth in population 64
  religious feeling 64–5
Golden Age of Armorica 3
Gourvennec, Alexis 131
governor 69
Great War 113–6
  agriculture, and 113
  allied troops 114
  Breton language, and 115
  cultural shock 114–5
  deaths 113
  Emsav 115
  industry, and 114
  strikes 114
Gregorian reforms 47–8
Guy de Thouars 42–3
Gwalarn 116

Henry II 40
  suppression of revolt by 40
  conversion to catholicism 66
Hill forts 7–8
Hisperic Latin 31
Homage ceremonies 55

Ille–et–Vilaine 7
industry
  aftermath of First World
    War 118–9
  Loire Basin 119
  post–war
    developments 133–174
intendants 71
Iron Age 4–5

JAC 118
Jacobin coup 1793 94
  Church, and 96
  overthrow in 1794 97–8
Jean I 44–5
Jean II 45
Jean III 45
Jean IV
  income 57
Jean V 53
  relationship with
    England 53
Jean de Chalon 59
Jean de Montfort 49–50, 51
  negotiations with
    English 51–2
Jeanne de Flanders 50
Jeanne de Penthièvre 50
Jengland-Beslé 28
JOC 118
John I 42–3
  Philip Augustus, and 42–3
Judicaël 24–5
Julius Caesar
  campaign against
    Armorica 8–10
    territorial boundaries 10
    Veneti, attack on 8–9

King Arthur
  popularity of legend 36–7

La Chalotais
  case against 81–82
La Villemarqué
  folk songs 111
Lambert 27–28

Lamoignon
  grand bailliages, and 82
Landois, Pierre 58–9
Le Balp, Sébastien 73
Le Gonidec
  Breton culture, and 110
Le Grand Peur 87
L'Heure Bretonne 125
Locmaria 21
Locmariaquer 11
Lorient
  creation of port 76
Louis XI 58
  purchase of rights to
    duchy 59
Louis the Pious 25–6
Louis the Stammerer 29
LVF 125

Magnentius 18
Maximus
  British immigrations, and 22
Mercoeur, duke of 65–7
Michel Le Nobletz 64–5
mineral wealth 15
missionaries 109
monasteries
  centres of culture, as 31–2
  expansion of 47
Morvan 25

Namnetes 6–7
Nantes
  economic success 75
  emigration to 103–4
  slave trade 75
Napoleon Bonaparte 99–101
  chouans, and 100
  education, and 99
  re–authorization of public
    worship on Sunday 99
  suspension of
    constitution 99
  war, and 100–1

National Constituent Assembly
  abolishment of all feudal
    rights 87
Nominoé 26
  Ballon, battle of 27
  Charles the Bald, and 26–7
  death of 28
  dux, and 27
  Lambert, and 27–8
  leader of Breton nation,
    whether 28
  national hero, as 26
  replacement of bishops 27
Normandy
  alliance with Anjou 39

Odet d'Agdie 59
Office Central des
    Associations Agricoles de
    Landerneau 117
Old Breton 31
Onion Johnnies 103
Osismi 6

Pagi 11
pardons 109–10
Parlement 54, 68
  administrative role 68
  exile to Vannes 74
Parti Breton 135
Parti National Breton 112, 116
  admiration for fascism 121–
    2
  Second World War,
    and 124–5
Pascweten 32–3
Penthièvre
  confiscation of lands 55
Pétain, Marshal
  attitudes to 126
Philip Augustus 42
  John I, and 42–3
Pierre II 53
Pierre de Dreux 43–4
  church, and 43–4
  excommunication 43–4

Pierre de Dreux 43–4 – *contd*
  increase of ducal control 44
  pact with England 44
Pippin III 25
pirates 17
pollution
  agriculture, and 132
population decline 57
population increase 103
post–war history 130–8
  agriculture 130–2
Poutrecoet 23
PPF 125

Questembert, battle of 33

railways, advent of 102
Ranulf de Chester 41
Rebellion of 1675 72
Redones 7
religion
  resistance to reforms 107–8
religions 16–17
Rennes parlement
  resignation 1765 81
  resistance to dissolution 83
Résistance
  activities of 128–9
Richard the Lionheart 41
Richelieu 69–70
Rivallon 39
RNP 125
Roman empire
  decline of 17
  prosperity of 17
  uprisings against 10
Roman Gaul
  administrative system 11
Roman gods 16–7
Roman roads 12–13,14
  trade, and 13, 14
Romanization
  extent of 15–6
Romanized rural
  settlements 12

Saint–Aubin–du–Cormier,
  battle of 60
Saint Malo
  corsairs 77
Saint–Sauveur de Redon
  monastery 32
Salomon 29–30
  Charles the Bald, and 29–30
  church, and 30
  conspiracy against 32
Salt
  trade in 7
Sant–Malo
  independent spirit 46
SAV 135
sea, exploitation of 56
Second World War 123
  Allied bombing 123–4
  Atlantic Wall 124
  Celtic Institute 129–130
  collaborationist
      parties 125–6
  cultural developments 129
  effects 123–130
  end of occupation 130
  fishermen 124
  food supplies 124
  German invasion 123
  PNB, and 124–5
  threat of, effect 121
Service du Travail
    Obligatoire 128
shellfish farming 133
Spain
  conspiracy of 1718, and 79
St Urnel–en–Plomeur
  burial site 20–1

taxation
  foreign woollen cloth,
      on 76–7
textile industry 75–7
  decline 105
tourism 110
  increase in 119
  post–war developments 134

Treaty of Guérande 51
    second treaty 52
TV Breizh 136

UDB 135
unemployment 120–1
URB 112
urban socialism
    growth in 117

Vannes 5
Vendée
    revolt 93–4
Veneti 5
    sea battle with Romans 9
Vichy regime 126–8
    decentralisation 126–7

Vichy regime 126–8 – *contd*
    Loire–Inférieure, and 127
    negative attitude to 128
Vikings
    Alan the Great, and 33
    occupation of Brittany 34
    raids after 908 34
Vingtième tax 80–1

War of Succession 49–51
    war of two Jeannes 50
Wigo 32–3
Wihomarc 25
William, duke of
    Normandy 38–9
Wrwhant 32–3